ACE CAFE

75 YEARS
1938 · ACE CAFE LONDON · 2013

▪▪▪▪▪▪▪▪▪▪▪▪ LONDON

WELCOME TO THE ACE

Petrol. Rock 'n' Roll. The Ace Cafe. Three simple expressions, but they represent the most powerful fusion, not only in yesterday's and today's bike and car scene worldwide, but also in tomorrow's.

Inspired by rich heritage and traditions, the spirit remains the same. The Ace still embodies the same values today as it did when it was built as a transport cafe in 1938, and which became a magnet for the Ton-up Boys (and girls) and Rockers.

What could be found on a Triton when going for the ton in the 1950s and 60s is emulated today on modern sports bikes and streetfighters.

Hosting all who share the passion, celebrating diversity and the difference, immersing into a culture with its own ethos – all combine to produce an addictive ambience and atmosphere that is to be both savoured and treasured and, when shared is simply the best.

It is with privilege and pride that we invite you to take a journey with us through the unique Ace Cafe London experience.

Mark Wilsmore

The innocuous transport cafe the Ace as it once was. These days it's hard to imagine when you are sat in the bustling cafe, eating a bowl of chilli and cheesy chips among a throng of bikers, but for years the Ace was just a transport cafe – originally built to serve those using the new A406 North Circular – tempting customers with a menu that included such delights as gammon and egg, or liver and bacon...**PHOTO:** ACE CAFE ARCHIVE

'LAZY SUNDAY AFTERNOON...

... I've got no mind to worry. I close my eyes and drift away-a...' Those lines from the Small Faces single Lazy Sunday (taken from the Ogdens' Nut Gone Flake album, released in May 1968) sum up the feeling of a typical day out at the Ace. Early morning ride in. Grab a hearty full English. And then chill with your mates, talking bikes – Classics, post-Classics, Choppers... whatever floats your boat. It doesn't get any better. *PHOTO:* MYKEL NICOLAOU

DST
67C

FBK
240

THE HEART OF THE ACE

An army marches on its stomach – and that applies to bikers, too. The Ace might be the ultimate meeting place for petrolheads in the world, but good old-fashioned British fayre is one of the big attractions. That, and carefully choreographed themed events so you can pick the meets that suit you and everyone who shares your interests. *PHOTO: MYKEL NICOLAOU*

ACE CONTENTS

ADDICTED TO SPEED

FROM TRUCKERS TO TON-UP BOYS

THE ROAD TO ACE CORNER

ROCKER STYLE

GO RACE TASTE THE ACE

BIKERS... AND THEIR BIKES

ACE TEAM

Editor: Gary Pinchin

Publisher: Marc Potter

Chief photographer: Mykel Nicolaou

Designer: James Duke

Production editor: Tim Hartley

Editorial contributor: Phil Mather

Photographic contributors:
Phil Masters, Ace Cafe London,
Iron & Air Magazine, Mike Cook,
Tim Keeton, Stephen Davison

Special thanks to:
Mark and Linda Wilsmore for their
enthusiasm in making this project

happen – and their passion that has
helped make the Ace Cafe so special.
George Tsuchnikas for his forthright
interview and enthusiasm for Ace business.
Hans Peter Rutten for taking his time to
get us up to speed with Ace Cafe Germany.
The guys at Iron & Air Magazine for
supplying pictures and words for
'The Road To Ace Corner'.
Derek Harris at Lewis Leathers for his

fabulous insight into Rocker fashion.
All the Ace Cafe staff for looking after
Mykel and I with cups of tea and chilli
cheesy chips during our visits.
And most of all, to the people we've
met at the Ace in recent months who
gave us the time to talk bikes and
allowed us to shoot pictures of their
wonderful motorcycles.
Cheers everyone!

Advertising key accounts manager: Steff Woodhouse swoodhouse@mortons.co.uk **Circulation manager:** Steve O'Hara **Marketing manager:** Charlotte Park
Production manager: Craig Lamb **Publishing director:** Dan Savage **Commercial director:** Nigel Hole **Managing director:** Brian Hill
Editorial address: PO Box 99, Horncastle, Lincolnshire LN9 6LZ. **General queries:** 01507 529529 24hr answerphone help@classicmagazines.co.uk www.classicmagazines.co.uk
Archive enquiries: Jane Skayman jskayman@mortons.co.uk 01507 529423 **Overseas distribution:** COMAG, Tel 01895 433600 **Printed:** William Gibbons & Sons, Wolverhampton.
ACE CAFE LONDON (ISBN:978-1-909128-04-0) is published by Mortons Media Group Ltd, PO Box 99, Horncastle, Lincolnshire LN9 6LZ UK

Member of the
Periodical
Publishers Association

Independent publishers since 1885

TON-UP COLLECTION

Any time you visit the Ace there's a small collection of bikes on display on the stage in the restaurant. The line-up changes from month to month – and the bikes are also used for outside roadshow events by the Ace. Some bikes are the personal property of Mark Wilsmore. Some are the property of the Ace. Some are supplied by a third party. But the one thing that all have in common is their affinity with the ethos of the Ace: the essence of speed and heritage of the ton-up boys and the rockers.....

WORDS BY GARY PINCHIN **PHOTOS BY** MYKEL NICOLAOU

ACE BIKES

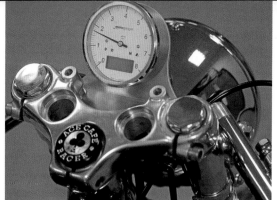

2013 ACE CAFE 1200 CR

HISTORY:

In 2008 when S&S Motors, the world's largest supplier of aftermarket American v-twin engines, celebrated its 50th anniversary, the guys there did so by inviting 50 of the world's leading custom builders to produce bikes using S&S engines.

Krazy Horse in Bury St Edmunds opted to build a cafe racer. Wilsmore's S&S bike was also a cafe racer, built by another UK-based custom house. The builders were subsequently invited to display their bikes at the S&S 50th anniversary party which is where Wilsmore

and Krazy Horse owner Paul Beamish cemented what has become a long-term working relationship.

With Krazy Horse moving to new premises this year, Beamish set about building a more traditional cafe racer and linked the build with Wilsmore to celebrate the 75th anniversary of the Ace and the 110th anniversary of Harley-Davidson.

The Ace Cafe 1200CR, as it's known, features a 1996 1200cc Sportster engine in a Wideline Norton Featherbed replica frame.

WILSMORE:

I've wanted to do a proper American-engined, Featherbed-framed cafe racer for years – ever since I saw a press cutting with a pic and few words that said American Lance Weil was making faithful replicas of the Norton Harley he raced in Britain in 1967. I called him in California and received a bumph pack... but the price of the bike was way out of my league.

So I've longed to have a Harley that goes and handles and stops – and that seemed to be it. We had a stab with Little Miss Dynamite – a bike built by a local custom shop, but while it looked okay from a distance, it wasn't right.

By the way, we named it Little Miss Dynamite in memory of Marta who died on a Reunion Run. She had Little Miss Dynamite painted on the back of her leather jacket.

So Paul Beamish used to come to the Ace because of his hot rod interest. He helped us out with bikes for events and between us we came up with the idea of this bike. We're doing a limited run of 11 – as its Harley's 110th Anniversary in the same year it's our 75th.

My notion is that there are 1000s of Sportster owners out there and there are loads of kits out there you can buy to turn the bike into a cafe racer. But they all look wrong, well, at least they don't look quite right. But get the kit right and you are away.

SPECIFICATION:

1200cc four-cam Harley-Davidson V-twin. S&S Super E carb with air horn and K tech enrichener. Crane Hi 4 single-fire ignition with single-fire coil. Stock Sportster five-speed gearbox and clutch. 2-1-2, polished stainless megaphones. Norley Wideline Featherbed style frame in T45 tubing gas bronze welded and nickel plated. Box-section swing-arm. 39mm Sportster forks with Progressive springs, rubber gaiters and Ace Cafe top nut. Harrison Billet six-pot caliper with stainless fittings. 11in Braking Wave disc. Twin Ohlins S36E shocks. Harrison Billet 4-pot caliper with stainless fittings. 11in Braking disc. Stock Sportster hubs with 17in alloy rims and stainless spokes. Avon Road Rider tyres (110 x 17in front and 150 x 17in rear). Aluminium 3.5 gallon sprint tank. Aluminium oil tank. Storz CNC rear sets. K-Tech master cylinder. Weight: 400lbs. Price: £22,000. Price with engine upgrades: £22,725. (Upgrades include: Wiseco forged pistons. Andrews N4 grind camshafts. Gas-flowed heads and roller rockers.)

1979 TRIUMPH BONNEVILLE

HISTORY:

On Any Sunday brought American flat track racing to British enthusiasts. The nimble-handling road-going twins, stripped down to become bikes suitable for the big fast oval flat tracks in the States, became as big an influence here as they were back home.

In the late Sixties / early Seventies flat track racing was a war between the Harley-Davidson factory and the British – notably Triumph and BSA, but also Norton. And as the sport had developed, and riders were looking for anything to give that little extra edge,

stock chassis were ditched, replaced with lightweight specialist racing frames and suspension.

But because the dirt ovals require a unique set-up and because the tyre rules have remained stagnant for years, one thing that's never changed in the look of a flat track race bike.

It's still as raw as ever... but with that glorious retro look. Hence the reason so many classic bike fans are continuing to turn to bikes such as Wilsmore's street tracker.

WILSMORE:

It was only after riding a Goldie, and then riding a Triumph, that I realised why the Bonneville was so successful. It's so quick off the lights and, when it was first introduced, must have been a revelation as the ultimate urban bike.

We all have a notion of speed and the epitome of that in the UK is the cafe racer that stems from our strong heritage of road racing. But in the States it's a very different story. Their equivalent to our cafe racer is the whole postwar hot-rod scene. But in terms motorcycling, it's all about flat track. I'd read about and seen On Any Sunday, but as soon as I saw it live, I started thinking 'I've got to get one of those on the road'.

But it was only luck that led me to this bike. Reg Allen's in Hanwell, Ealing is my nearest shop and I was having a cup of tea and a good yak with Bill Crosby – the shop owner. There was this T140 in a racing chassis – proper classic. The engine had been tuned, blueprinted and he asked me if I was interested in it. I said I wouldn't mind it as a flat tracker. Turns out the guy still had the original frame. Bill owns one of the old Strongbow Triumph flat track bikes they built in the 1970s – it's in the National Motorcycle Museum – but he knew I wanted something that looked similar.

By the time the bike was built, we were full on into sorting the Ace out, hence the black and white checkers on the yellow paint! The thing is a bastard to start but is a mental wheelie machine. It's a scream of a bike to ride. But we've been so busy with the Ace I've not ridden it much since I stripped it down to rebuild it.

SPECIFICATION:

Triumph T140 air-cooled, parallel, overhead valve, twin-cylinder, engine. Twin Amal Mk.II carbs. Duplex, mild steel, tubular frame. Twin shocks, Oil-dampened forks with Micron fork brace. Twin Lockheed front calipers and discs. Lockheed rear caliper and disc with AP master cylinder. Right-side mounted twin exhausts with Campbells 'cocktail shaker' mufflers. Akront rims 18in 2.15-40-S front, 18in 2.15-40-S rear. Avon Super Venom tyres 100/90/V18 front, 120/90/V18 rear. Cut-away primary casing. Box-section swing-arm

1962 BSA ROCKET GOLDSTAR

HISTORY:

The Rocket Gold Star, combining the pre-unit 650cc A10 engine in a Gold Star-type frame, was only produced for 1962 and 63, replaced by the unit-construction A50 and A65 twins that had been launched in January 1962.

The RGS engine was based on the A10 Super Rocket with a light alloy cylinder head and sporty camshaft but, for the RGS, compression was also bumped up to 9.0:1.

It featured magneto ignition and an Amal Monobloc carb. The bike produced 46bhp at 6250rpm.

The frame was similar to the double-cradle Gold Star – but without the kink in the lower left-hand frame rail to accommodate the oil pump on the Goldie. Forks were also Gold Star. Rear units were Girlings.

But there were also a lengthy list of aftermarket options for BSA and other suppliers to give the machine additional performance – and even more radical looks.

WILSMORE:

My Rocket Gold Star is the epitome of 'ton-up' at a particular moment. Being immersed into the whole Ace thing, there had to be one of those here – although I have to admit, I've only done a few miles on this particular machine.

There's a never ending and ever changing list of things we love. For me I love to put context and visual to the iconography that is 'ton-up' if I get an opportunity and this bike tells the story. A Fireblade, for example, is a far superior machine but that's a very different story.

In reality, I'm deep set with age and I'm a Triumph man. I love the whole Meriden thing and all the foibles that come with the bikes that came out of the place, but the Rocket Gold Star is of its time.

I got this bike from Len Haggis Classic Motorcycles and while it's in relatively stock trim there are some nice touches, like every little goodie Eddie Dow produced damper, top yoke, and rebound damping which is arguably a big improvement, a finned rocker feed and the rather nice twin-leading-show front brake.

I believe the Rocket Gold Star, launched in 1962, was the epitome of the BSA twins – A10 Super Rocket engine in the Gold Star frame. Not only was it fast, it handled superbly.

The 650cc A65 unit construction twin superseded the pre-unit motor, but to my mind the A10 engine was (and still is) a thing of absolute beauty, especially wrapped in the glorious Gold Star styling.

SPECIFICATION:

Air-cooled, parallel, overhead valve, twin-cylinder, engine. 70mm bore x 84mm stroke, 646cc. Amal Monobloc carb. Lucas competition magneto. BSA Gold-star-type double-cradle frame with swingarm. BSA Gold Star forks in Eddie Dow 'Superlegerra' yokes and headlamp brackets.
Dunlop WM2 2.5 x 19 front rim with Avon Speedmaster tyre. Dunlop WM2 2.5 x 19 rear rim with Avon tyre. Smiths Chronometric speedo and rev-counter.

WILSMORE:

This started for our 70th anniversary when there was an approach from the racing organisation Bemsee (The British Motorcycle Racing Club). It was its centenary and our 70th, so a tie-up was proposed. The suggestion was us backing a one-make race series for Triumph Thruxtons, which we were well up for. Bemsee said Tony Scott would deliver it but as the year progressed Tony wasn't comfortable with the prospects of trying to fill a grid at a time when the nation was in financial meltdown. So we came up with a brilliant alternative – a street version of the bike we would

have raced. Tony Scott Racing took it to the nth degree on race-prepping a street bike. It's like yesteryear with modern tech and it's transformed the bike into a missile.

We own this demo model and we've sold eight replicas. When you've ridden a stock Thruxton and then ride this one you keep asking yourself: 'how the heck did they manage to squeeze that much performance out of the engine and chassis?' It's an absolutely brilliant bike. I've ridden it to Germany, raced it, ridden it back home and enjoyed every single minute of it.

2008 ACE 904 THRUXTON SPECIAL

HISTORY:

The Ace 904 Thruxton Special was borne out of a collaboration between T3 Race, Ace Cafe London and the Stonebridge Motor Company to bring together the classic days of 'record racing' along with the nostalgic feeling of that time. All mixed with modern thinking and materials it produced a very special motorcycle, styled to perfection and engineered with excellence. Tony Scott, of T3 Racing, the creator of the machine, pledged that this would be a very limited edition run with only 15 models being produced. This was because the components used to create the machine from the Triumph Thruxton EFI would be designed and built from scratch using only the best materials and engineering by companies with pedigree.

SPECIFICATION:

Air-cooled, DOHC, parallel twin, 360 degree firing order. 90mm bore x 68mm stroke to give 904cc. Compression ratio 9.9:1. Fuel injection with SAI Transmission. Wet multi-plate clutch. Five-speed gearbox. Tubular steel cradle frame with tubular swing-arm. T3/Nitron 43mm upside-down forks. T3/Nitron twin shocks with piggy-back reservoirs. Twin 310mm full-floating wave front discs with T3/ISR six-pot monobloc caliper and radial master cylinder. Single rear 255mm disc with Nissin two-piston caliper. 17x3.5in alloy front spoked wheel with 120/60/17 tyre. 17x 5.5in alloy rear spoked wheel with 160/70/R17 tyre.

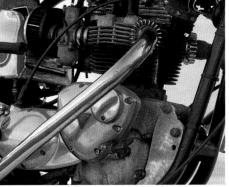

WILSMORE:

If you look back there's a natural evolution. Manx, Goldie, Rocket Goldie, Triumph Bonneville. Then someone had the brainwave to stick a Triumph engine in the Norton frame. I've had this Triton a long time. Since the 1980s. Bill Crosby at Reg Allen built it for me – but it was not until I'd passed what felt like a 20-year test that he took the Norton frame off the wall for me.

He said: "You get an old motor and we'll see what we can do." I found one advertised in a local small ad and

when I went to see about buying it there was a container full of old Triumphs. The guy had imported a pile of ex-police bikes from South Africa but they were all in various states of dismemberment. I bought one, but only for the engine – a 1977 T140 Bonnie.

I'd also bought a rare Bonneville cylinder-head – it was a 'factory' centre-plug racing head. I'd also bought the coolest front brake I'd ever seen – a CMA four-leading shoe. Being that proved to Bill I was 'worthy'. So this is the real 'special' of my collection.

1977 TRITON T140

HISTORY:

As Wilsmore points out, the Triton was a natural progression to the young rockers of the Sixties looking for more performance from their Brit bikes. The Norton Featherbed was considered one of the best handling bikes on the road while the twin-carb 650cc Bonneville motor, in pre-unit and later unit construction form, was more suited to tuning for speed and acceleration than the Norton twins of the time.

The Triton, initially perhaps the preserve of the racer or even home builder, spawned specialist hybrids like the Seeley, Dresda, Rickman – all three companies with a rich racing heritage. Plus there were plenty of firms offering bolt-on goodies to ensure the cafe racer look – including John Tickle, Paul Dunstall, and Ian Kennedy.

SPECIFICATION:

1977 Triumph T140 air-cooled, parallel, overhead valve, twin-cylinder, engine with factory-spec central plug cylinder head. Twin Amal concentric carbs – parallel inlets. 1950 Norton Wideline Featherbed frame with Dresda box-section swingarm. Norton Roadholder forks with CMA four-leading shoe front brake. Alloy Tank Shop fuel tank. Central oil tank and battery holder. Akront 19in 1.85-40-S684 front wheel with Avon Venom tyre 100x90-19in. Rear Akront rear 18in 2.15-40-S692 rim on Triumph conical hub with Avon Roadrunner rear 110x90H18. Smiths clocks. Matador levers. Tomaselli twist-grip and headlight brackets. Gold star pipes, swept back headers.

WILSMORE:

The Rickman? It's an evolvement of the Triton thing. In the cafe racer narrative the Rickman is part of the story. As much as I'd love to ride bikes like this, I don't get the chance. Maybe that's a good thing. You don't have to sail on HMS Victory to understand. You can just look at and imagine. You'd get more of an idea if they gave you a bowl and a biscuit with weevils – but I doubt you'd choose to eat it and really immerse yourself in the experience. Maybe that's how it is with the Rickman. Having said that, the Rickman story is fantastic – how it came to pass that a small company,

for a short period, was the only kind of volume producer of the British motorcycle industry. Last man standing.

I think it took the whole cafe racer thing to another level in terms of engineering development.

And Rickman also deserves credit for helping keep the British motorcycle industry afloat. At one time it felt like this were the only manufacturer still producing bikes.

And the red and yellow livery? It just reminds me of the Isle of Man TT emblem. When you add it all up, everything is a perfect fit.

1974 RICKMAN T140

HISTORY:

Derek and Don Rickman were scrambles stars of the late 1950s and early 60s. The Metisse name (French for mongrel), was coined after they modified their own race bikes. By 1960 they produced lightweight frame to house Triumph or Matchless engines and earned considerable off-road success in America and Europe. In the mid-60s they built similar lightweight frames for road racing and in the 1970s turned their attention to road-going machines with frames kits – with distinctive lines and nickel-plated frame tubes – for several engines including Triumph, Honda CB750 and Kawasaki Z1. They also produced their own large-diameter forks and undertook engine development with an eight-valve cylinder head to fit Triumph twins.

SPECIFICATION:

1974 Triumph T140 air-cooled, parallel, overhead valve, twin-cylinder, engine. Lightweight chrome-moly tubular, duplex black-painted Rickman frame with nickel-plated swing-arm. Rickman forks. Twin Lockheed front discs and calipers. Lockheed rear disc and caliper. Borrani WM2 alloy rims with Avon Roadrunner 4.10H19 front tyre and Dunlop TT100 4.10x 19 rear. Smiths clocks. Chrome reverse megaphones with alloy ends.

WILSMORE:

I'd say of all the bikes I own, the one I've ridden the most is the TR65 Thunderbird – one of the last-gasp Meriden Triumphs. It's conked out a few times but apart from that, and the normal consumables, it's been fantastic given the environment I live in.

The single carb engine offers a really nice, smooth power delivery. It's only got a tiny fuel tank, but this is as Triumph intended, and is quite economical too, so it's no big deal. And with those America bars, I always found it easily manoeuvrable in traffic.

I used it every day for everything for about 20 years – work and social. At one time I had a 30 mile commute and

it was perfect for that. It was my daily ride until Triumph kindly loaned me a bike.

The thing is that riding the Thunderbird so much hones your senses for not just the road environment you are in, but also to the bike itself. It helps keep you on top of things mechanically... but what I found, as I added bikes to my collection and spent time riding different bikes each day, is you don't take on board the maintenance issues the bike tells you it needs like a daily rider does. I have a TTS as well – another last gasp Meriden bike. It was a noble concept and had great punch but was kind of still-born.

1982 TRIMPH TR65 THUNDERBIRD

HISTORY:

The TR65 was a product of the workers co-operative at Meriden, re-introducing the Thunderbird name to the Triumph range in 1981. Production lasted until 1983.

It was a single-carb, short stroke version of the T140 Bonneville, but while it was produced in US spec with high bars and smaller two gallon tank, the model was never exported to the States due to emission rules.

Instead it was aimed at the economy market in the UK and Wilmore's bike is thought to be one of a batch of nine in production when Meriden closed in August 1983. Roebuck's Motorcycles, Rayner's Lane went to Meriden to finish the bikes and sold this one to Erica Jones. After 22,000 miles in nine months, she sold it to Reg Allen who in turn sold it to Wilsmore.

SPECIFICATION:

Air-cooled, parallel, overhead valve, twin-cylinder, engine. Amal concentric carb. Duplex, mild steel, tubular frame. Twin shocks, Oil-dampened forks. Single hydraulic disc front brake, drum rear. Chrome swingarm. Dunlop TT100 4.10/H19 front on chrome rim. Dunlop TT100 rear tyre 4.25/85H18 on chrome rim. Veglia clocks. Lucas electrics.

WILSMORE:

You don't have to ride this bike to enjoy it. I can sit with a cup of tea and just get so much pleasure from looking at it. The Brough name means a lot of things to a lot of people. I'm old and if you are of a certain age you can appreciate everything the Brough Superior stands for. It's what a Spitfire means to an RAF person. It stirs so many emotions. I'm English and I thoroughly enjoy our history and heritage. Sadly, in my opinion, it's something we overlook far too much. When you look at the Brough it conjures images of Lawrence of Arabia and his bikes (Lawrence owned eight Broughs and had a ninth on order at the time of his death). It's Noel Pope at Brooklands and Bonneville. So much heritage.

And it's absolutely brilliant that Mark Upham has set up in business to resurrect manufacture of the Brough Superior, using modern engineering methods to build new machines, but with all the old style. Long may it continue!

But for me, the Brough respresents a very important element in our motorcycle heritage.

2010 BROUGH SUPERIOR S101J PENDINE

HISTORY:

Brough Superior motorcycles were made by George Brough from 1919 to 1940, marketed as high quality, high performance machines and were dubbed the Rolls-Royce of motorcycles.

Each machine was tailored to the customers' demands and every motorcycle that left the Haydn Road, Nottingham workshop was thoroughly road tested. Estimated total production is thought to be 3048 machines, the top of the range SS100 powered by a JAP or Matchless overhead valve v-twin and being certified as having a top speed in excess of 100mph.

Rights to the Brough name are now owned by Mark Upham who continues to produce machines to the same high standard originally established by George Brough.

SPECIFICATION:

SS101J air-cooled, 50 degree V-twin, two valves per cylinder, 86mm bore x 92mm stroke to give cubic capacity of 1150cc with an 8.7:1 compression ratio. Three-speed gearbox, NEB clutch. Tubular steel frame. Castle forks. Tapered head races. 21in wheels.

WILSMORE:

I've been fortunate to have had every Street Triple model that Triumph has made. Fortunately, the guys there have taken pity on me destroying so many beautiful old bikes and given me their lovely new machines over the past few years. I think it's safe to say the Street Triple is 'idiot Wilsmore proof!'

Every three years, when the MoT is due, they take the bike away and have given me a new one to replace it. This latest one has brutal raw power. And over the years the Street Triple has evolved into a street fighter and is spot-on for the environment I ride in. It's my daily ride now.

It's light and nimble so I can flick through traffic and, like the old TR65 Thunderbird, is perfectly suited to my environment.

But if I felt so inclined, I could ride it to the Nürburgring and have a great time thrashing around the old road course there, with confidence that it would perform up to the task of being ridden to its limits. However, whether or not I still have the mettle to explore the absolute limits of a bike that's this good is an entirely different question!

2012 TRIUMPH STREET TRIPLE

HISTORY:

Since its introduction in 2007, the Street Triple has been a massive hit, fusing the style and attitude of the iconic Speed Triple with the performance and agility of the class leading Daytona 675 supersports machine. The result is a truly impressive middleweight streetfighter that has attained critical success around the world. The torque and sound of the liquid-cooled 12 valve triple, combined with a close-ratio six speed gearbox produces an exciting, exhilarating ride that made the Street Triple Triumph's best selling model since its launch.

SPECIFICATION:

Liquid-cooled, 12 valve, DOHC, in-line three cylinder. 74mm bore x 52.3mm stroke. 675cc. Fuel injected. Wet multi-plate clutch. Six-speed gearbox. 105bhp 78kw at 11700rpm. Two piece die-cast, aluminium beam twin-spar frame with twin-sided cast alloy swing-arm. KYB 41mm upside-down forks. Twin 308mm floating front discs, Nissin two piston sliding calipers. KYB shock. Single 220mm disc with Brembo single piston caliper. Cast alloy five spokes wheels, 17x 3.5in front with 120/70 ZR17 tyre, 17 x 5.5in rear with 180/55 ZR17 tyre.

classicbikeshows.com

PRESENTS

THE FULL THROTTLE TOUR 2013/14

OCTOBER 19-20, 2013

The 20th Carole Nash Classic Motorcycle Mechanics Show – Stafford County Showground

OCTOBER 31-NOVEMBER 3, 2013

The International Dirt Bike Show – Stonleigh Park

JANUARY 4-5, 2014

The Carole Nash Classic Bike Guide Winter Classic – Newark Showground

FEBRUARY 8-9, 2014

The Carole Nash Bristol Classic MotorCycle Show – Shepton Mallet

APRIL 26-27, 2014

The Carole Nash International Classic Motorcycle Show – Stafford County Showground

SEPTEMBER TBC, 2014

The 21th Carole Nash Eurojumble – Netley Marsh, nr Southampton

OCTOBER 18-19, 2014

The Carole Nash Classic Motorcycle Mechanics Show – Stafford County Showground

Tickets online at www.classicbikeshows.com
or call 01507 529529

ADDICTED TO SPEED

Mark Wilsmore is the ultimate petrolhead. His high-octane lifestyle is fuelled by a passion for fast bikes, road trips and rock 'n' roll. He loves seeing other petrolheads enjoying similar indulgences. But he's also a great organiser. And those credentials have made him the driving force behind the Ace Cafe. This is his story... and that of the Ace Cafe re-birth...

ACE INTERVIEW

WORDS BY *GARY PINCHIN*

Mark Wilsmore is the epitome of Ace Cafe culture. He wears an open-neck fleece emblazoned with Ace logos. His straight-cut jeans have just enough turn-up to reveal his footwear to be engineer boots. Strategically dangling out of his back pocket is a black and white checkered bandana. Always.

The hair is slicked back. He's clean-shaven apart from the sideburns. He puffs the thinnest of roll-ups. And he constantly uses the terms petrol, speed, demographic, tribe and culture, whenever he talks.

From the appearance, you don't even need to speak to him to realise he is of the 'rocker' era. Maybe not by birth. But definitely by design.

It's not just for show. He's 100% biker. The daily commute on a Speed Triple is one thing. But there's also massive road trips across Europe or America. Mark lives the dream. And the dream is the rocker lifestyle and everything it entails.

What's more, his passion has driven him to providing a home for thousands of other like-minded petrolheads to follow their dreams. That home is the Ace Cafe.

The Ace is 75 years old this year. Located in Stonebridge, north west London, it was opened in 1938 by Vic Edenborough to serve as a transport cafe off the then-new A406 North Circular road.

By the Sixties, the Ace, thanks to being open 24 hours a day, had become a mecca to the new breed of ton-up kids – a place to hang out, drink a cuppa and jive around to the rock 'n' roll sounds on the jukebox.

Mark's too young to remember those heady days though: "I'm not old enough to have come here when the Ace was in its heyday," he said, "but I am old enough to recall the era.

"I was born in 1957 and recall a childhood that was very much influenced by motorbikes. My life seemed filled with noise, drama, excitement. From about seven years old, all I can remember is British bikes. People in black leather jackets. Mods and rockers. My best friend at primary school had an elder brother who was a full-on mod and had umpteen scooters. I used to think they were really cool."

While Mark yearned to be part of the action, he had no inkling of the pitched battles between

the mods and rockers of that time. "I learned to ride a scooter in a field but hung out with lots of people older than me so I knew lots of people with bikes, and some of them raced. Motorcycles were all around me. Summers consisted of seeing mods and rockers filling amusement arcades but I had no idea of the animosity between the two opposing tribes."

Mark's mind instead was full of ideas about owning a motorcycle. Having a major motorcycling event on his doorstep cemented the notion.

He said: "In 1966 we lived in a village near Woburn Abbey – and it was the year of the BMF Rally, as it was once called, being held there. I remember seeing thousands and thousands of bikes everywhere. The noise and drama of all of that. Loads of people in black leather jackets. I wanted to be part of it."

But if his father had had his way, Mark would have never got involved with the two-wheeled fraternity.

"My father – I don't recall him as a policemen because I was too young at the time – was a policeman. We lived in a police house so there were people knocking on the door at all hours, day and night. Invariably a lot of the calls were about bike crashes, bikes losing it over the Grand Union Canal on the A41 as I remember it.

"He came home one day to say: 'You are not going to ride a motorbike'. There was always this undertone. But boys, being boys, my younger

brother and I wanted to do the most exciting thing in life we could think of – and that was riding bikes.

"You try lots of things as kids. I remember going fishing and sitting there thinking, 'why do people do this? It's so utterly boring'. That was crossed off the list of things to do.

"So was football. My age group was overwhelmingly full of smoothies, suedeheads and all that was wrapped up with football. I was bored senseless with that – although I loved the vibe of a big crowd to an extent. Luton was our nearest team but I went to West Ham once – no real connection at all, but it seemed like it might be an exciting thing to do. But football just didn't click with me in my early teens."

But Mark had ridden a scooter – and enjoyed the same kind of music that the scooter boys – the mods – listened to.

"I enjoyed the music of that era that the skinheads and smoothies listened to. But the thing was, and I don't know why, but I really loved rock 'n' roll. At the youth club rock 'n' roll would come on and always, at end of evening there'd be a punch up. I was only 14 at the time but you can imagine the 19 and 20 year olds would be there with their bikes parked outside. And then they'd roar off on the North Circular. Yeah, I wanted a bike."

Mark worked at a local bike shop to earn a few shillings by cleaning motocross bikes. But it was

there he realised that the mechanic's side of things wasn't for him. He just wanted to get out and ride.

Yet he was prepared to wait for the pleasure. In December 1971, the Tory government brought in legislation that forced 16-year-old motorcyclists to ride mopeds in what history shows to be an ill-fated effort to reduce accidents.

"At 16 we could get Fizzies or other 'peds but that was of no interest for me because it didn't stack up with Gene Vincent and black leather jackets. You'd trip over a copy of *MCN* and read about Barry Sheene or Agostini and think, 'I want to be like him'. Why would you ride a moped?

MEANEST, FASTEST

"When I turned 17 I bought a brand new bike – a 250cc Yamaha RD250. I'd venture I did like many – I went to a local dealership, that sold Yamaha and that's all it sold. But I'm sure if it had sold Kawasakis, I'd have bought a Kawasaki. At 17 it wasn't about buying something retro – I just wanted the meanest, fastest thing I could lay my hands on with the money I had. It wasn't about retro then."

Mark discovered that it was one thing going fast on a motorcycle. Staying on two wheels was another and he experienced a series of accidents – though none failed to curb his enthusiasm, and addiction for speed.

"I can't remember how long I had the

Yamaha. It wasn't long. I'm trying to recall the order of my crashes…" He pauses to count them… "But I certainly wound up in hospital soon after getting it. I also remember destroying a mate's 250 Suzuki too. He came to my school but came from Bedford – where there was a Suzuki dealership. I can't remember which bike I'd crashed but ended up with a broken shoulder and my arm hanging out the front of my body."

But the motorcycle had given Mark the freedom he was looking for.

"Having a bike meant whizzing around, doing your own thing, finding your own way. That's how I ended up in Southgate, at The Royalty Rock 'n' roll Club – loads of older teddy boys, rockers, plus a whole swathe of my age group too, dressed in checkered shirts, turned-up jeans, Lewis Leathers and flat top haircuts. That was the rockabilly group. And that's when I realised I wasn't on my own (in my interests)."

Mark came to British bikes very late – even though he aspired to owning one.

"I always loved the sound of a British bike and the look. But the compelling thing at the time was to get the fastest thing I could afford. Having a bike meant I could go to Silverstone to see Barry Sheene race too, but stood behind the chicken wire, miles from the track, you could see bugger all. It was just about the ride there and back in packs of bikes – that was the real reason to go.

"The passage of time and good fortune to be able to earn money means I've bought other bikes. But I've had loads of crashes too. My brother totted it up and reckons I've spent five years of my life in hospital through motorcycle crashes.

"With that interest… I joined lots of different clubs and ended up in loads of different clubs. I joined the 59 Club but you gradually learnt it's not just a badge but it is a place. You go there and realise it's hallowed ground. Somehow though, whatever I did or wherever I went, I was the youngest and just missed out on the real scene as it was – or came to it too late.

"I used to whizz around, getting stopped for speeding. I used to get stopped every day by the police and had to produce documents to the police station on a regular basis. Including the idiot local policeman who even knew me, he came from the same place. He knew my name but I was just practise for a new copper… nothing's changed today I'm sure."

FIRST BRIT BIKE

As can be seen, one of Mark's traits is veering off track as he recalls some tale or other loosely related to the initial topic. It makes for him being a great raconteur, able to hold court with the best when it comes to the social history of biking culture.

And getting back to British bikes…

"Oh yeah. In 1981 I bought my first British bike, which I still have. It was a brand new

Triumph Thunderbird I bought during the last gasp days of Meriden. Maybe it's just as well Triumph went to the wall because it then gave rise to the brilliant bikes we have coming out of Hinckley today," he suggests with a view that may well rankle traditionalist fans of the Meriden marque, even if it is probably closer to the truth than others might like.

"The Thunderbird broke down in the first week," he chuckles, "and I used to get through so many 'consumables' but in the bigger picture, I rode it every day – to work and to play! But owning that led me to joining clubs.

"By then, I'm a serving cop and in my peer group there's a smattering of people with whom I share the same everyday uniform, but where I was posted there was a lot of youngsters on sportbikes of the day and one slightly older colleague riding a Brit bike to work. The younger lads would all take the piss out of us on the British bikes.

"But in the social group I belonged to outside of work there were packs of us off to the races. We'd go to the Dutch TT and Bol d'Or and, for some reason, it always fell to me to organise the ferries and the route.

"We had some terrific journeys with quite an eclectic mix of people – young policemen out of this country riding like they were Barry Sheene and a tribe of us riding like the clappers on old British bikes. It was great times but in essence I

was 'Mister Organiser.' And as time went on, the group got bigger and bigger. We had 30 people on a trip one time and all sorts of things come out of that: Crashes, people off to hospital, how to get them or their bikes home."

It wasn't just about riding the bikes. Mark had always had an interest in history – "History and geography lessons were the only time you'd find me at school," he said – and he was becoming increasingly interested in English history the more he rode around the countryside.

"Among the social group with those of us on Brit bikes and wearing black leather jackets, as much as I like hot-rods, big fins and Elvis, as time progressed, I became acutely aware of our own English heritage. I could see buildings going (being pulled down). History being ignored, all swallowed up by development. I'd go to Brands – but only as an excuse to go to Johnsons. Sadly that disappeared. I'd go to the 59 Club and found I was immersing myself in cultural history. I don't want that to sound pompous, but 'immersed' is the right word.

"Strange thing is that I've lived down the road from the Ace for 30 years. So I'm very familiar with this stretch of road. Very familiar with this building. But most of that time the Ace was a tyre depot. I can't recall it as a cafe but I feel sure that my dad and I drove by it when it was.

"When I look around, everywhere it's an onward march of McDonald's, KFC, plastic America. It's so clichéd – yet arguably isn't real America anyway. Yet here we are with our own fantastic heritage."

ACE REUNION

With that in mind, it's easy to understand how, when the call to action came, Mark was at the forefront of a plan to save the Ace Cafe. But it came in the most unlikely way.

"Tail end of 1993 I was in the West Middlesex Triumph Owners' Club and this chap came to me – he's quite a bit older than me and knows me as being a bit of an 'organiser' – and said: 'do you know when the Ace shut?' He knew my interest in rockabilly etc., but I couldn't give him an answer.

"The guy said: 'It was 1969'. Big smile on his face. 'So?' 'Well, think about it. C'mon, think about it.' I counted on my fingertips and thought... ah... light bulb came on. 1994 would be 25 years since the Ace shut. And the moment I realised that, another little bulb came on. Reunion.

"From that moment, in my mind, we'd do it. I had in my head pretty quickly how to do it and who would help. That was put to bed and in very short time I'd moved on from that to thinking, 'hang on, that reunion could be the key to re-opening the Ace'. From that moment, that was the mission. Reunion first, then move heaven and earth to get the place reopened.

"So I took on the task of organising it. I was

thinking, 'we'll have to get a book done on the history of who we are, and why we are. And maybe a film on the back of that'. I shared my thoughts with people and they came back saying, 'how can we help?' and suddenly the whole thing had this momentum.

"Some older guys were a bit negative, saying, 'why bother, what's the point?' but that just motivated me to try even harder to show them why.

"So having chased that and started to figure how to re-open, I had to make stark choices. Almost immediately I knew I didn't want a museum. I wanted it alive. People enjoying it."

Mark focused on research, talking to countless people, many of whom had previously frequented the old Ace. He also talked to Courtney Edenborough, whose father Vic had opened the Ace back in 1938.

"Courtney was a mine of information but the more you talked to people, the more you understood the dynamic of the place," he said. "So while I didn't want a museum, my conviction was that it must retain the spirit. And there was a stark realisation that although the bikes had changed quite dramatically since the early days, the spirit of the Ace hadn't. We knew we could still make the Ace a place for people interested in petrol."

The reunion took place at the site of the Ace, with some 12,000 bikers turning up.

"It was a massive success but was almost too big. To steer attention away from the Ace I

deliberately organised the 1995 reunion at Jacks Hill Cafe on the A5. I didn't want to prejudice any planning permission by having thousands of bikers descending on the site (and causing traffic chaos). In 1996 we held it at Brighton."

All this time, Mark and his wife Linda were working on plans to re-open the Ace.

The biggest challenge was how to re-open it and operate as a business venture. Mark didn't have that kind of background.

"There certainly wasn't a Haynes manual on doing that," he laughed. "We needed to secure the building first so no one else could get their hands on it. Then we'd need planning permission. And I didn't have a clue about who could help bring that about, but in the passage of time you work towards that and gradually get there."

At that stage the Ace Cafe site was a tyre-fitting depot and Mark worked on buying the freehold.

"We bought a period of two years whereby the freeholder agreed not to sell it. So we had two years to sort the planning permission and finances to go through with the purchase. Just as the two years was ending, permission came through for us to go ahead with plans for the cafe.

"In that time I'd also worked on raising the money and that basically came down to robbing the family! My brother and our two wives were the original shareholders. Having purchased the freehold, we then discovered that our tenant (the tyre depot) had renewed its commercial lease for

25 years. And its rent paid the mortgage."

The tyre depot didn't open Sundays, so the Ace did. Mark got someone in with a van to sell burgers – a brand new van, in Ace livery that was on site every Sunday at 6am.

"Loads of bikes turned up, which was great, but we soon had the hot rod crew asking us to open for them too and we eventually held Hot Rod Night on a Wednesday evening.

"Not surprisingly we had loads of other different groups all wanting their own special night so the next thing was to work out, how to do the real deal. How to re-open the Ace as a cafe. Not a museum, but a fully fledged operating cafe."

BLOWN WATER MAIN

The catalyst came in the most unexpected form – the water main explosion on March 6, 1999. When that blew it flooded the entire area, closing the North Circular for days. But the explosion also devastated the building.

"The water company was obliged to put the building back to normal but my thought was that this was now the time to re-open the Ace as a cafe.

"That's when we brought in other directors. I'd met George Tsuchnikas in 1995 and we'd talked over a plan for the Ace. We both agreed then it had to be a working cafe. George, plus Wayne Huff, Nick Law and myself formed the board of directors for the Ace.

"I'd met Wayne in 1993 when I was planning the Ace Reunion. I was in contact with Screaming Lord Sutch, who has since become a good friend, and told him my plans and he said I should contact Wayne, who was a film maker. Wayne looks after the business side of things.

"Once we got talking, Wayne said his wife knew George who, at the time, was the operations director of the Grand Metropolitan Group (which ultimately merged with Guinness in 1997). He never actually launched a company but was brilliant at taking a restaurant or brewery company and relaunched it. He knew nothing about bikes – but he knew all there was to know about running something like the Ace – from the point of view of the restaurant business. Bear in mind at the time it was just a shell of a building, post water main explosion, but had everything mapped out in his head for the format of the Ace.

"And Nick is a property man – a commercial surveyor – who I've known for years. Then there's my sister who is an accountant.

"They are the team behind the Ace. I can ride bikes but I'm useless as a mechanic. Similarly I like to think I know what makes the Ace tick but I've no qualifications to run a business. It's this combination of people that makes the Ace work. A perfect management team."

Mark's inital thought was that with a new road being built parallel to the existing Ace the access round would steer traffic away from the tyre

depot and it would only be a matter of time before the company would ask to break its lease.

But it was the burst water main that changed everything and it was the Ace approaching the tyre company to buy it out of its lease!

"With hindsight there is no blueprint to something like this. It's bloody obvious. If you are into petrol, where do you meet? Then it's down to giving all the different groups what they want. It's like all kids want is a bowl a chips – older people want something more substantive."

With the Ace almost an immediate success story, you might think that other old cafes might jump on the bandwagon and regenerate, but the reason for the success of the Ace isn't just down to Wilsmore's vision – at least that's what he says.

PETROL COMMUNITY

"I suppose I did to a certain extent expect some kind of reaction from other cafes in England but the beauty of the Ace is its location and its heritage. We're on the edge of a population of 8-10 million people. But ultimately it's the combination of facets that make the Ace work. It's not just a place for the petrol community to come at night. There's a daytime business too and without it, the Ace just doesn't stack up. You need all the elements for a successful business. Let's face it, it's a cafe with a huge car park on the edge of London. And the reason it is a success now, as it was years ago, is down to its location."

But it's more than that drawing people, not just wanting to visit the Ace. It's not just the people who frequent the place. There's a worldwide affiliation to the Ace. You only have to look how many bikes bear the Ace logo. Or how many bikers sport Ace badges on their leathers.

And even beyond that, it's the huge diversity of tribes within the petrolhead community that frequent the Ace. Why is this?

Mark said: "It's recognition that the Ace is a place for petrolheads – and not just for bikers. There's a realisation (from Mark's standpoint) that the different demographics of those who love petrol needs to be managed. And that comes in the form of not mixing age groups. Organising the nights just fell into place really. It's a case of knowing who wants what. The craft is the knowledge of realising what fits what night the best – what tribes fit with other tribes."

Of all the great events that Mark has overseen since re-opening the Ace, there's one moment that he cherishes the greatest.

"It has to be the first cup of tea we sold from inside the building when the Ace reopened. It was to Stevie Andrews, an old mate of mine."

If you visit the Ace you will invariably see Mark, as busy as ever. It's a vocation he enjoys, so what does he get out of running the place?

"I just like to see people enjoying themselves. If I can do that, then it's a privilege for me. Seeing people enjoy this place, enjoying their

vehicles. But the brutal reality is that it has to be a commercial success."

With that in mind, comes talk of the future. There's talk of an Ace Cafe site in the States. Another in Germany. A host of outside events.

"We are compelled to branch out. If you don't, you sink. It's how society works now - either grow or you die. It's unfortunate but that's how it is.

"The costs here (at the Ace) are forever increasing. There's always new legislation to comply with and that always costs money. There's always a drought somewhere so food costs keep escalating. And the reality is that the service opportunity here (the ability to get people through the door to buy food) is finite. It ain't rocket science.

"But it's fun going to other places, meeting new people (so expansion is a good experience). The future of the Ace has the same ethos – it's built on speed. And the philosophy is to enjoy it.

"We look forward to opening a branch of the Ace in the States. There's a huge population, much vaster than here in the UK, but while they have a strong heritage of motorcycling out there, it's nothing compared with the car heritage to draw from. You can imagine they won't just have hot rod nights. It'll be Ford Hot Rod nights. It'll be brand specific because they have so many people into petrol out there. And plans are still formulating for a site in Germany.

"The future is looking really interesting. I'm certainly looking forward to it."

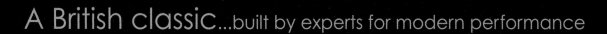

Above:
George Tsuchnikas with the brand logo that he's helped take worldwide

Opposite top:
American racing fraternity at the Ace! Left to right: George with Triumph racing chassis building legend Rob North, Mark Wilsmore, two-time AMA National champion Gary Nixon, Daytona 200 race winner and former BSA factory rider Don Emde and Tony Scott of T3 Racing in the UK

Opposite bottom:
George (left) with Mark McKee (Ace licensee and representative North America) and Mark Wilsmore

ACE BUSINESS

THE ACE

AS A BUSINESS

For most of us who go to the Ace Cafe – it's a place to meet like-minded enthusiasts, admire interesting bikes, drink tea, eat great food. But behind the lifestyle brand, lies a solid business foundation. Ace co-director George Tsuchnikas is also the operations director and, as such, looks after every aspect of the business side of the Ace. Who better to give the lowdown on how the place operates – and how Ace Cafe London is capitalising on a brand that has become a worldwide phenomenon...

First of all George, please tell us about your background in business.
I came to England 33 years ago, having worked as a chef on cruise ships. In England, I worked in pub restaurants – my wife Susan's family had pubs, hotels etc. Susan and I became managers for Scottish and Newcastle and then I spent five years in developing brands and restaurants for Grand Metropolitan, which is where I gained most of my experience in the food and restaurant trade. Susan and I also opened our own businesses in Southport and Preston – Italian-style cafe bars – and, in the mid 1990s, we also had our own consultancy business, advising others how to make their way in the food and restaurant trade.

How did you meet Mark Wilsmore?
It was February, 1995. I met with Mark as a favour to a friend who told me that Mark was thinking of trying to reopen the Ace and needed some advice. In time we became business partners and in 1998 we bought the freehold to the Ace and reopened the cafe in September 2001. The rest is history.

You're both coming to the Ace from very different backgrounds though?
Mark has a passion for motorcycles, rock 'n' roll and had a vision to bring the Ace back to life. My passion is very much the business angle. I'm food and drink. But for 14 years I was also one of the directors in the Sefton Chamber of Commerce, two years as chairman. It's now part of the Liverpool Chamber of Commerce.

At the time, some might have said you were both taking on a massive project in trying to reopen the Ace.
I think every year that goes by proves that Mark was not so mad in his desires because we've shown the Ace Cafe works. Maybe it's shown I'm not so mad also for supporting him! It's amusing and amazing to realise that the toys Mark played with when he was younger (the cafe racer motorcycles) are once again popular worldwide.

How is the business structured?

Mark and I are two of five directors. All of us have specific roles and experience in what we do. We have regular board meetings once a month to drive the business forward. That is very important. Mark is very customer and brand orientated. And I've never met anyone who is a better networker than Mark. He's always thinking about how he can help others – always introducing people who he thinks may be able to help each other in business – not just for the Ace, but for the benefit of the two separate parties. He's also great at generating ideas. I'd say out of 10 ideas he comes up with I only pursue half of them – but only because of time demands.

Will we see more Ace Cafes in the UK?

There is only one mecca. Ace London is the focus in the UK and we have no interest to open anything else in the UK.

But there seems to be a sudden flurry of Ace Cafe franchises opening for business around the world. Why now?

We're organically grown. We had to mortgage and it's only now that we're coming to the end of that period (of the mortgage). We know we have a safe, sound business and that has allowed us to consider licensing in other countries. There's no 'for sale' sign, or licence sign. People approach us. We get so many enquiries.

Tell us about Ace Cafe America?

We have a partner in North America and we've been talking for four years. We have secured premises in Orlando, Florida and we're hoping the first American site will open there next summer.

You also have Ace Cafe Finland.

It's a small representation of the Cafe. We call it Ace Corner and it operates as a rockers' cafe. Its location is beautiful, on the side of a lake, 100km north of Helsinki and it hosts regular bike meets.

ACE CAFE ♣ 37

Ace Germany has been a travelling road show for some time now. Will it have a permanent site at some time?
We've worked some time with our licensee, Hans Peter Rutten – he's been looking after Ace merchandise in Europe since day one and is currently aiming to propose a new Ace Cafe permanent site in Northern Germany (see pages 102-104).

Mark has always said the Ace is a place for petrolheads and he always talks of the cafe's heritage. We understand Ace Germany, Ace North America and Ace Finland because all those places have a strong history of motorcycling. How does the Ace philosophy square with Ace Beijing?
Ace Beijing opens its doors in 8-12 weeks. With China being such a highly populated country, Beijing opens the road to the East for us. We have four licensees in Japan representing the Ace in brand and fashion. So up to now it's been a merchandising company but we are now looking at creating Ace Cafe Tokyo. But to answer your question, China, plus Thailand, Vietnam, are like Britain was post Second World War. There are growing numbers in motorcycles and cars and Ace Cafe is not just about motorcycles – it's petrolheads.

There's so much going on for you guys. How do you see the future of the Ace Cafe – as a brand?
Ace London gets many enquiries about licensing and we treat them all with the same formula. Out of 10 maybe one, or two maximum, get beyond a second or third email. The reason we don't continue the discussion is that the interested parties either lack funds, lack a suitable location, or lack a sound business plan. I don't think people realise it takes seven or eight years of planning to open the doors – or to find the right people to open the doors. And it takes five really committed directors to keep the thing afloat. It really is hard work but when you have something as special as the Ace Cafe, then it's worth all the hard work to see the business grow – but more important, to see the customers so happy.

ACE WORLDWIDE

The Ace Cafe is well-established in the UK at its site on the North Circular in London but it has become a worldwide brand. That's not been achieved by chance. Every year the Ace Cafe attends events all over the world. Last year alone, the Ace Cafe was represented at numerous major motorcycle events worldwide. And there are now licensees operating in five different countries, working to promote Ace Cafe in its respective territories. The map gives some idea of how global the Ace Cafe now is.

EVENTS ATTENDED

1 Milan International Motorcycle Exhibition (500,000 visitors)
2 Verona Motorcycle Expo
3 Madrid Mulafest
4 Rome
5 Intermot, Cologne
6 Helsinki
7 Petersen Automotive Museum, Los Angeles
8 Barber Festival, Alabama
9 New York
10 Intermot, Munich
11 Glemseck 101, Stuttgart, Germany
12 Paris (twice)
13 Ace Cafe Exhibition Isle of Man TT

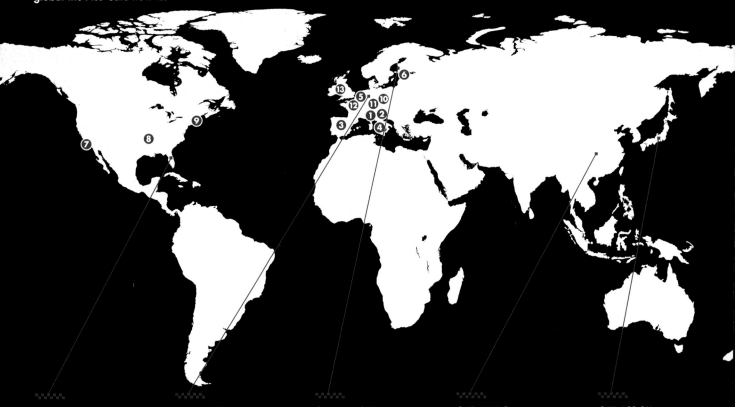

ACE USA
Licensee and representative
Mark McKee
Premises to open in Orlando summer 2014
www.ace-cafe-london.com/usa.aspx

ACE GERMANY
Licensee and representative
Hans-Peter Rutten
Still seeking premises and hopes to announce details in 2014
www.acecafelondon.de

ACE FINLAND
Licensee and representative Riku Routo
Premises 'Ace Corner Finland' open and operating with a 'Rockers Restaurant'
www.ace-cafe-london.com/finland.aspx

ACE CHINA
Licensee and representative
Yulun Qu
Premises to open in Beijing this winter
www.ace-cafe-london.com/china.aspx

ACE JAPAN
Licensee and representative
Sachiko Okayasu
www.acecafelondon.jp

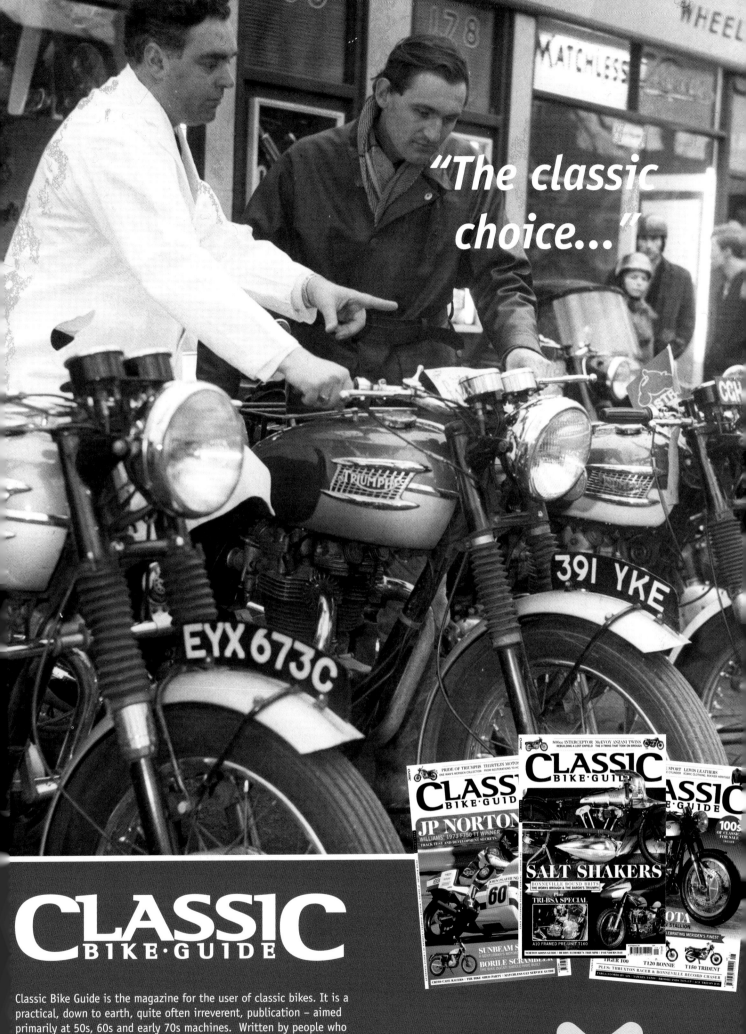

FROM TRUCKERS TO
TON-UP BOYS

Transport cafe. Garage. Aircaft engineering works. Car wash.
Home to motorcyclists. The site just off Stonebridge Park station
on the North Circular saw some massive changes in the three
decades from its opening in March 1938

WORDS BY *PHIL MATHER* **PHOTOS COURTESY OF** *ACE CAFE*

I n the March 1938 issue of, *The Bedford Transport Magazine*, the journal of the Bedford Drivers Club (BDC), reported on the opening of the Ace Cafe in glowing terms. "With a frontage of 350 feet and one of the largest lorry parks in the country," the new building boasted all mod cons including central heating, and toilets for both ladies and gentlemen with hot and cold running water.

The kitchen, although hidden from public view, was tiled throughout and fitted with the most up-to-date equipment more commonly found in a luxury restaurant. It was staffed efficiently too, able to provide fast service for as many as 100 drivers at a time, 24 hours a day. And most importantly, despite all the newness, the Ace Cafe maintained 'coffee stall prices'.

The Ace was more than a cafe though. It joined a list of around five hundred BDC 'approved' drivers' rest houses situated up and down the country, providing essential rest and relaxation facilities to the truckers who laboured day and night, fetching and delivering goods along what was in many places an unforgiving road network. There were no motorways in prewar Britain, and no ring roads to divert through traffic from the bottlenecks of town and city centres.

The drivers' needs had been recognised by the BDC, but for a long time a roadside tea shack and an unofficial forty-winks in the cab at a lay-by (although illegal since 1933) was all many had to look forward to in terms of home comfort. Now the Ace offered easy parking, a games room with a dartboard and billiard table, and most importantly a bed with clean sheets for the night. As many commented, there were times when life on the road was a lot better than being at home.

If the concept of the Ace was relatively new, then so too was the road alongside which it had been built. The UK's problems of ever increasing motor transport, the upkeep of existing roads and the creation of new ones had been cause for concern from the early part of the 20th century, but any solutions were put on hold by the outbreak of the First World War.

With the return to peace, the British Government created a new Ministry of Transport, and the 1920s saw a series of schemes implemented to create major arterial roads radiating out from London, with a North Circular Road around the top edge of the capital to channel traffic around the conurbation. The A406, to give the 'North Circ' its official title, was over 12 years in the making and eventually linked the A4 to the west at Chiswick with the A12 to the east at Wanstead. It was mostly single carriageway and in places ran through what was then open countryside, but at its western end, where it was spanned by the Grand Union Canal aqueduct and several railway bridges, it was split into two carriageways with a grassed central reservation.

The improved road system encouraged new building, particularly industrial development, which together with the proximity of main railway lines at Stonebridge, was to play a fateful part in the Ace Cafe's history. Infill housing was going up alongside the new factories, but what to put on a relatively small patch of land sandwiched between the new road, the River Brent and the railway, and the Northfield Industrial Estate, was puzzling the owners. To entrepreneur Vic Edenborough the answer was obvious. He had already built-up two small cafe businesses from scratch and knew that a combination of hard work, good service and advantageous location (his Halt Cafe was opposite the bus depot in Hendon) was the key to success. Now he was ready for a more adventurous scheme – the vacant plot beside the main road was the ideal location for his envisaged ritzy transport 'pull-in'.

THE FIRST ACE

'Road House' seems an apt description for the squat, rectangular building dominated by its high pitched roof. It was set at an angle to the road so that approaching drivers would have no trouble spotting the raised fascia with its Ace Cafe refreshments sign, illuminated with neon at night. An art deco-style electric clock was added above the fascia (advertising Smiths new 'Sectric' electric clocks) serving as a quick reminder to passing travellers that they had time for a quick cuppa and helping lorry drivers who had to keep track of their driving hours on their log sheets.

The enterprise was an instant success, no doubt much to the relief of the builders and the company that had supplied the catering equipment on extended credit, prompting Vic Edenborough to push forward with another plan, the construction of a garage and petrol filling station alongside the cafe. The Ace Service Station opened the following year, in the summer of 1939, offering fuel from a line-up of pumps on a forecourt island, new and second-hand car sales, servicing and repair.

If postwar performance is anything to go by, business at the service station may well have outstripped the cafe in a very short time, but Great Britain declared war on Germany at the beginning of September and life at the Ace changed forever.

Private motoring became severely restricted by fuel rationing and undertaking journeys not deemed essential was frowned upon. However, the workshop facilities at the garage didn't stand idle – they were extended to create a machine shop which undertook work for the Ministry for Aircraft Production and extra bodies were drafted in to do the work. The cafe was ideally suited to serve as a workers' canteen and at night it became a watering-hole for passing convoys.

Unfortunately, the location of the Ace Cafe placed it on the edge of a Luftwaffe target area. Hendon, with its concentration of aviation and general industrial targets, and the Willesden railway yards, had been earmarked for destruction before the war had begun, and bombing accuracy being what it was, it wasn't long before the Ace was damaged. Within nine weeks of the commencement of German night-time raids in September 1940, the left-hand end of the building was hit, demolishing the end wall, blowing out the front windows and bringing down the roof.

The clock stopped at 4.30. A temporary pre-fabricated building was erected which allowed the cafe service to continue, but the building itself had been dealt a fatal blow.

When the Blitz came to an end in May 1941, much of the rubble from the damaged buildings was transported to the Twyford Tip, a rubbish dump on the south side of the North Circular between the Stonebridge Park railway bridge and the Grand Union Canal aqueduct – directly opposite the Ace Cafe. In some places the dump was 50 feet high and at its northern end it spilled onto the south-bound carriageway of the road, effectively blocking that arch of the railway bridge.

Left:
The ton-up style of the day: Jet helmets were a modern innovation replacing pudding basin lids. Note the Vinnie couple with matching gear.

Below:
Love is: ton-up, two-up on a Triumph twin.

'Bombing accuracy being what it was, it wasn't long before the Ace was damaged. The left-hand end of the building was hit, demolishing the end wall, blowing out the front windows and bringing down the roof above. The clock stopped at 4.30'

THE NEW ACE

After the war, what remained of the old cafe was knocked down and wheelbarrowed across the road. While the service station was updated with re-equipped workshops, a car showroom, a 'Washmobile' car wash (reputedly the most modern in the country, although not cheap at five bob a throw) and additional petrol pumps, plans were drawn up for a new cafe along modern lines.

Whether the idea came from Vic Edenborough himself, or London architects Westmore and Sanders who undertook the design work, the building followed the style of Streamline Moderne that had become so popular in the late Thirties with American gas stations and roadside diners. It was long and low (the first floor at the back was added later), the front wall was almost entirely of glass divided by five slim brick pillars, the facia was bordered above and below by horizontal lines, the roof was flat and a pylon, or tower, at one end was adorned with the cafe name and a modernist clock face. Incongruously, a rounded corner section on the right featuring porthole windows, which appears on an original architect's drawing, was transformed into an angular kiosk with shuttered openings for selling ice cream, and a rather unattractive, box-like extension was added on the left to accommodate a restaurant area.

Inside, the counter ran along the back wall with rows of table and seat units, enough to accommodate 90 settings, at right-angles to the front windows. These units were a triumph of function over comfort. The hard plastic seats with low backs were fixed to a single central pedestal underneath the tables by horizontal supports; to enable a person to sit at the table the seats swivelled around. The design made for easy cleaning and sweeping the floor without the impediment of table and chair legs, but nobody could sit on the hard plastic seats for long.

DECLINE AND CLOSURE

Thanks to Vic Edenborough's Midas touch, the new Ace Cafe, when it opened in 1948, became a hive of industry, employing 25 staff and serving as many as 2000 meals a day. The early Fifties were undoubtedly the Edenborough Empire's heyday, with a non-stop stream of customers travelling by on the North Circular boosting profits to the point where two more local service stations were purchased, and then in turn the service station side of the business was sold to Lex Garages Limited. Yet despite high aspirations, the Ace Cafe remained primarily a transport cafe, or 'caff' as everyone called them, and the need for a restaurant area, eventually sidelined for special events, dwindled as private motorists sought out more salubrious places to dine.

At the same time, a new class of customer was emerging. Motorcycling was increasing in popularity in the UK and, in turn, motorcyclists often turned away from pubs, were on the lookout for places to meet, to ride to and to recover in after a journey in more often than not inclement weather. Somewhere that provided a mug of hot tea and a plate of egg and chips, and didn't mind you sitting down in a wet and dirty motorcycle oversuit.

WASHMOBILE
CAR SHAMPOO FROM FIVE SHILLINGS

'As time went by a pattern emerged – a group would come together through shared interest, hang out for a few years, then disperse. Another group would take their place, drawn together by the same interests, outwardly similar but subtly different in their choice of dress, music and the machines they rode'

The Ariel Owners Club held its inaugural meeting at the Ace Cafe in November 1951, and the AJS & Matchless Owners Club was set-up the following January. Less formal groups, formed by friends or workmates, chose the Cafe as their meeting place and gathered there before setting off to a race meeting at Brands Hatch or a visit to the seaside at Southend or Brighton. Or they simply got together in the evening for a run to another caff like Ted's Cafe in Chingford or the Busy Bee on the Watford Bypass.

As time went by a pattern emerged – a group would come together through shared interest, hang out for a few years, then disperse. Another group would take their place, drawn together by the same interests, outwardly similar but subtly different in their choice of dress, music and the machines they rode. National Service scattered many, as did the responsibilities of work, marriage and parenthood. And occasionally somebody would lose their life.

LIVE FAST. DIE YOUNG

Towards the end of the Fifties, the rising number of deaths among young motorcyclists, their alienation from mainstream society through appearance and behaviour, and their seeming disregard for the law and safety attracted the attention of a national magazine, *Weekend*, which published a sensationalised story woven around a fatal accident at the Iron Bridge bends, about a mile-and-a-half from the Ace heading east.

The fact that by now Ace folklore dictated that the bends should be taken at speeds between 80 and 100mph didn't help matters. Neither did the coroner's report that stated that there was no doubt in his mind that at the time of the crash a race was in progress.

Weekend reporters interviewed riders at the Ace, as did journalist Royston Ellis whose radio documentary 'Burning It Up' was broadcast on BBC radio in January 1961, shortly before the publication of his 'Live fast, love hard, die young' expose in *Today* magazine. Further bad publicity for the Ace came in an episode of prime time television's Dixon of Dock Green screened by the BBC four days later, to be followed by a 'shock issue' feature in the *Daily Mirror* leading with the front page headline 'Suicide Club!' splashed above an obviously staged photo of a ton-up boy thrashing his Royal Enfield around the car park. That only left the local police to top things off by steaming in mob-handed that Friday and arresting 20 or so miscreants for 'insulting behaviour' after they jeered at a police car.

The Ace Cafe limped on for a further eight years. The number of lorries pulling-in dwindled as the once free-flowing North Circular itself became congested with the ever increasing weight of traffic, and rigid enforcement of a blanket 40mph speed limit by police drove the bikers away. There was trouble of a more serious nature too – *The Guardian* of September 28, 1969, reported that a motorcycle gang had turned up at the Ace the day before and smashed bottles, cups and chairs. On Bonfire Night, November 5, the year before, petrol had been poured across the road and then set alight, halting the traffic. Possibly to avoid similar incidents, the Ace Cafe lights were turned off and the door locked on Tuesday, November 4, 1969.

Unbeknown to all but a few, the show was finally over, the Cafe had closed for good. Such a shame that in the final years, as journalist Graham Forsdyke wrote in *Motor Cycle*, you "began to notice the cracks in the cups, the weak taste of the coffee and the grease on the chips". Such a shame, too, that the only spoon for stirring your tea at the counter was secured by a chain to prevent anybody nicking it and that the jukebox had been surrounded by a steel cage to prevent a repeat of somebody tying a rope between it and the back of a parked lorry 'for a laugh'.

ROCKERS:
HOW WE GOT THERE

If Ace Cafe boss Mark Wilsmore was on Mastermind he'd max out the history questions. In particular, he has an incredible knowledge and understanding of social history. Specialist subject? Biker culture. This is his view on how we got to where we're at, in terms of ton-up boys, mods and rockers…

You know that when you are 18 you will be called up for National Service. So you grow your hair, you earn some money, you buy your bike and then think 'okay, I'm going to have a good time because they're going to stick me in the Army soon…'

SOCIAL HISTOR

Postwar there was the baby boom. On one side you had people who felt really guilty about the millions who had died between 1939 and 1945. On the other side you had people who were glad it was all over. And everyone was busy rebuilding devastated communities.

So out of the baby boom came these young lads who missed out on the war. It was a terrible period for those who lived through the Second World War, but these kids growing up postwar had little going for them. They wanted some action.

They earned only a little bit of money but then came the advent of credit. In the UK, all these young kids could afford was a motorcycle. In the States it was cars.

At that time, there were no speed limits outside the towns. So there were fast roads – and on those fast roads were coffee bars and truck stops. The music playing in the coffee bars – and the milk bars in the towns – was rock 'n' roll. It was played in daylight remember. And kids used to dance around to it.

So you had the cafes, the rock 'n' roll – and the speed on the bikes.

Suddenly the carnage on the road goes up...

If you look back to the photos of that era from the motorcycle shows, it's all young kids. Yes it's the old boys in glasses and suits puffing on pipes running the stands, but the vast majority of the public are these young kids.

There was no training. No L-plates. No speed limits. And the coolest thing in your life if you were a teenager was to own a motorcycle.

You wore an old flying jacket – so you looked like one of the Second World War heroes. And the next bit of kit was your crash helmet. You stuck that under your arm and looked like one of the new jet-age pilots. You're hard now. A proper tough guy.

All this carnage is reported in the local papers. The nationals don't have time for it. They've more important things like The Suez Crisis.

So between the local press and the magistrates, these youngsters start getting labelled as ton-up kids... Once you label a generation with contempt, that generation will turn around and go 'yeah, I'm a ton-up kid' and try even harder to live up to the tag.

Then the 59 Club opens as a youth club. It's a place for kids to go to listen to music. The 14-year-olds tell the organisers to bring the ton-up boys along because these youngsters all aspire to owning bikes too. It's that death or glory thing. It's the spirit of youth.

But by now the carnage is so bad on the roads that in January 1962 an episode of Dixon of Dock Green sets out some contemporary advice. It was a weekly TV drama depicting the Met Police but it was used for moral lectures on aspects of local crime.

This particular show is all about carnage on the roads and Dixon (played by Jack Warner), this wise old police sergeant, talks of the 'lunacy of some lads on the road' and bemoans how their wild antics on bikes are getting lots of lads killed. Not only that, mentioned in the programme is that the Ace Cafe is where all these ton-up lads hang out.

So now this has become a national agenda. Three weeks later, the front cover of the Daily Mirror calls it a 'suicide club' and demands something be done to stop the carnage.

The furore that follows culminates in a government investigation, which sets the scene for a national limit that is implemented in 1963.

But in 1962, Father Bill Shergold comes to the Ace to hand out leaflets to motorcyclists, inviting them to go to the 59 Club for a blessing of the bikes. It's his way of trying to calm the lads down a bit.

At this stage these lads are still not identified as rockers... That didn't come until 1964 – again courtesy of the media.

Imagine you are one of the 14-year-olds from a working class background. You know that when you are 18 you will be called up for National Service. So you grow your hair, you earn some money, you buy your bike and then think: "Okay, I'm going to have a good time because they're going to stick me in the Army soon..."

You do your two years' National Service and by now you've got a bit more cash so you come out in 1963 and go and buy yourself a Bonnie and think you are a right Jack-the-lad.

But if you are 14 in 1963 the dynamic has changed. You're now more middle class. A bit more affluent. But bikes have become relatively expensive. Along come the Italians and offer some crazy promotional deals on scooters.

You are already listening to modernist music (beat music influenced by African American soul and Jamacian ska) and you are spending your money on the new fashion of tailored suits.

And now you can afford a scooter. With the latest Carnaby Street fashions you are a sharp-dressed man. And mobile.

In 1964 you and the boys ride down to Brighton on your scooters on Bank Holiday Monday. When you get there the ton-up boys are already there on their bikes.

This, remember, is the first time in history that an entire generation has their own transport. Before, you'd have either gone to the seaside with your mum and dad or stayed at home.

But there are two distinct groups – distinct by age group, clothing and method of transport. And what's more, the aspirations of both groups are different. You've your working class ton-up boys and then the modernist middle class who wouldn't dare get their hands dirty.

They meet on Brighton front and all hell kicks off.

When the press get hold of it, they like labels. The ton-up boys listen to rock 'n' roll. "Aah, they must be rockers."

So the ton-up kids go: "Yeah, I'm a rocker..."

So there you have it: mods and rockers.

The interesting thing is that this all applies to the States – but with cars. You had the traditional hot rod fraternity – the working class who stripped down their old cars to the bare bones and tuned up the engines. And then came the Ivy League college kids with their new saloons.

The whole shift is well documented in American Graffiti. Although it was made in 1973, the film is set in 1962 with the lead character bemoaning the demise of the hot rod – and how the new cars and music are not his world.

The story lines might be different with American Graffiti and The Leather Boys but both relate the same cultural changes.

Then in 1967/68 America, through president Lyndon Johnson, was trying to express its hope for the future following John F Kennedy's assassination. All JFK's ideals had been lost in the Vietnam war so there was revolution among the middle classes there. You had the Prague spring. The Czech revolution. Colonels were running Greece. Portugal was ruled by a dictator. There was the Paris uprising and the western world was on the verge of change.

But all the middle classes kicked back. You suddenly had the backpatch (outlaw) clubs and the hippies taking drugs, all trying to forget about fighting. Suddenly, Western society became infatuated by the mysticism of the East. The Beatles met Ravi Shankar. People wore Afghan coats, and took drugs. Everyone said 'peace man'. And the hippy bikers in the UK tried to emulate the American bikers with apehangers and sissy bars – trying to live out a more laid-back lifestyle.

SUICIDE MACHINE

In 1961 the *Daily Mirror* sensationalised the supposed rockers' penchant of dicing with death. In 2012, the Ace became the custodian of the decaying remains of the Royal Enfield that made the cover story.

The media often loves to paint a picture of someone behaving badly and when motorcyclists hit the headlines for all the wrong reasons. A spate of serious crashes – some fatal – among rockers gave Fleet Street plenty of ammunition to writing damning headlines, condemning motorcycles.

One particular headline appeared on the front page of the February 9, 1961 issue of the *Daily Mirror*. It shouted: Suicide Club and pictured the biker supposedly flat out on his 700cc Royal Enfield Constellation. Except the picture was stunted up outside the Ace.

Years later, when the Ace was in the throes of being re-opened, Mark Wilsmore met the owner. Wilsmore picks up the story: "We had a burger van before the cafe re-opened and this fella came along and said he'd been at the Ace years before. He pulled out of his bag a copy of the *Daily Mirror* and said: 'that's me on the cover'.

"He said he'd sold the bike but out of the same bag he pulled out his leather jacket he'd been wearing when the *Mirror* did the picture. It had a skull and crossbones painted on the back and I thought then, it seemed like the earliest example of the skull and crossbones being used as part of the biker imaginary that I'd seen.

"He told me: 'Everyone said that it was so dangerous being a biker back then that I thought I'd paint the skull and crossbones on my jacket'.

"He wanted to loan me the leather jacket to display in the cafe but we'd just had the huge water leak (after the mains burst and flooded the area) so I told him I had nowhere to store the jacket and gave it back to him.

ACE HISTORY

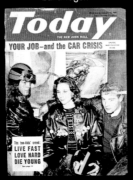

"We agreed that I'd have it once we'd sorted the cafe out... but I never saw him again and I've since lost his contact details. Months later though Roger, another older mate of mine – one of the old ton-up boys and an original Ace Cafe local – got talking and I said it was a real shame about the jacket... and an even bigger shame that he had sold the bike.

"Roger looked at me and said: 'He's not got it because I have! I've had it for years. I must get it done up some time.' I asked him not to sell it without giving me first shout. 16 years later I was still saying the same about the bike to him.

"Sadly, Roger died in 2012. It was the first time I'd experienced one of my peers passing on and I have to say I found it a very harrowing experience. At his funeral his wife said Roger always wanted me to have the bike. It was a fantastic sentiment for her to say that. But I couldn't just take it. And I had no idea what it was worth so I went to look at it that winter.

"I was astonished how many bikes Roger had – and it was quite funny because all the bikes were in chronological order of breaking down – the oldest being at the back of the shed. The Enfield was in there with Tritons and other Brit bikes.

"I picked Eric Patterson's brains and Alan's at Hitchcocks (the Enfield specialist) to arrive at a figure that would not embarrass me or Roger's widow. Hence the bike came here, and as an object that has a direct reference to the Ace Cafe it has an incalcuable value."

Daily Mirror

2½d. Thursday, February 9, 1961 • No. 17,775

SUICIDE CLUB!

● **It devours 130,000 members EVERY YEAR ! !**
● **See Pages 3, 13, 14, 15 and 28 today ! ! !**

CHARLIE WILLIAMS

I was born in 1942 and started going to the Ace in 1958/59 at 16½ years old when I bought my first bike – a 500cc Triumph Tiger 100. There were no laws then to restrict you. You bought what you could afford and I think I paid £130 for it, second–hand of course. It was a lot of money then but I'd been saving a while because I desperately wanted a bike.

I used to live in Bushy and a friend up the road from me had a bike. He was about 10 years older and had a Triton – his dad had been a motorcyclist too – and I used to talk to them and just got the bug.

Right near my home was the Busy Bee on the A41 and we all used to hang out there and then ride out to Windsor, Boreham Wood and of course the Ace. I suppose there were about 15 of us in our group at the Busy Bee – seven of us all lived within 500 yards of one another. We'd meet at the Busy Bee, have a drink and decide where to ride to.

We'd do Brighton or Southend of an evening, let alone a Sunday. We'd finish work at 5pm, meet at the cafe at six, ride down to the coast and then be back at 10.30. It was something to do of an evening – and great fun. Weekends we might do Brighton, but then we also used to go to the races at Brands Hatch or Silverstone.

I still ride with the Busy Bee crew – and have done so since the club formed in 1999/2000. I'm looking forward to our annual reunion at the Hilton on the Watford bypass that's held on the site of the old cafe on the first Sunday of every September.

Back in the Sixties the places we hung out at were all transport cafes but the Ace was just that little big different. I don't know what made it feel that way. Maybe it was just somewhere new for us to go, young lads exploring, but we'd hang out there, some nights till midnight, and then have to be ready for work the next morning.

We had some great times but while I've heard all the stories about people racing down the road and back to beat the single on the jukebox I never saw many people doing that. We just used to spend time chatting and then head off somewhere else.

The Ace was a cafe but it was the music and people that really made it special. I used to work all over London so I got to know a fair few people and meet them in Ace.

After I'd owned the Tiger 100 for a couple of years I part-exchanged it for a 350 Goldie. A year later I bought a 500 Goldie but swapped that for a Matchless G45 racer for the road. Then I built a Triton, using a Bonneville T120 engine in a Manx frame.

In 1966 though I bought another 500 Gold Star, one built in 1960, and that's the bike I still ride now (as is pictured left). It's had bits done here and there to it over the years but is about as original as you can expect it to be after all this time. I've got a FZ1000 Yamaha, which is way more comfortable to ride – the Gold Star is a pig by comparison. Let's face it, it is years behind in technology compared to the Yamaha but I have to say, the Gold Star still does it for me. It's got its faults. It's really lumpy, as you'd expect a big single to be, but I still love riding it and I get out on it about once a month.

I went to the 59 Club too when Father Bill Shergold was there. I remember joining up with the 59 Club for a ride up to Blackpool. I suppose there were 20-25 bikes that weekend.

I was at the Ace when they filmed the Leatherboys (movie) and was actually in one of the clips – the lead rider leaving the Ace. In the book, the Ace Cafe, Now and Then, they've quoted me talking about the Ace saying: "The Ace was tea, chips and speed…" I was at the Busy Bee when Michael Caine was being filmed too.

I went to the Ace off and on until it finally closed. By then people weren't going so much anyway and I'd stopped too because my job had changed and that alters your circumstances. When it finally closed, it was just the way it was. The Busy Bee closed the same year and whether there was something going on behind the scenes politically I've no idea.

When the Ace re-opened, first as just a tea hut in the car park and then as the cafe, I rode there on my Gold Star. It's a really good venue and Mark (Wilsmore) and his wife Linda have put so much into making it work. It must be really difficult in these times to make a success of any business.

It's still a great place to go and I still enjoy being there on a Sunday, meeting up with a few friends for a chat. It's not what it was 50 years ago but then you can't expect it to be. The young people have a different outlook than we did but they still do the same things – ride their bikes and hang out at the Ace.

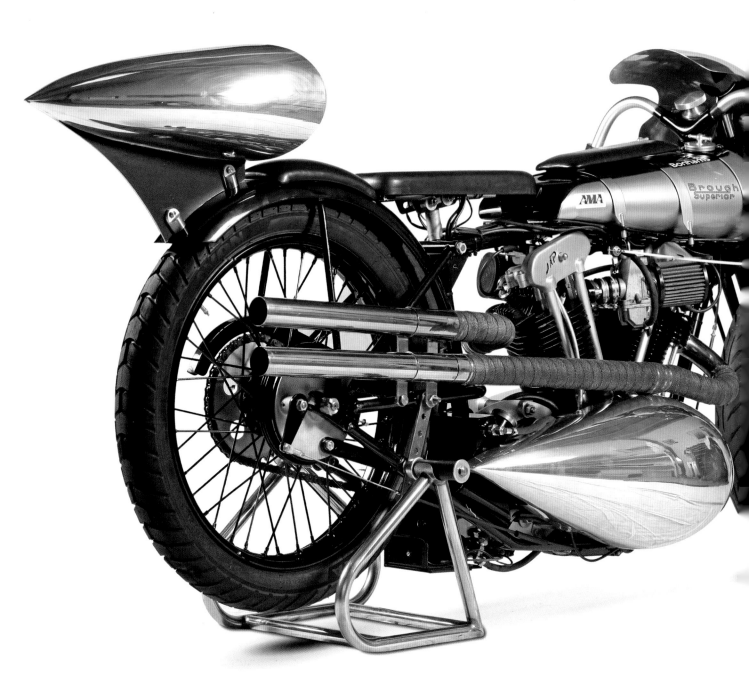

THE NEED
FOR SPEED

It's all about going fast. And there's nothing like the speeds
recorded at Bonneville. Ace Cafe is linking up with the official
Brough Superior team for another assault on the famous salt flats

WORDS BY *GARY PINCHIN* **PHOTOS BY** *MYKEL NICOLAOU*

ACE BONNEVILLE

onneville. If you're a biker then its significance is the iconic Meriden-built Triumph twin. But if you're as much of a speed junkie as Mark Wilsmore, its significance is far greater.

The Triumph earned its moniker after Johnny Allen set a new motorcycle land speed record of 193.730mph, riding a Triumph twin-powered streamliner in 1956 on the Bonneville Salt Flats, near Wendover in the state of Utah.

The salt flats are the largest of several in an area located west of the Great Salt Lake and have earned worldwide notoriety by hosting motorsport events since 1912 – with the first-ever land speed record being created in 1914.

Bonneville hosts two major land speed record events each year and the Ace became involved when Brough Superior made a successful return to the Salt Flats in 2011 at the famed BUB Speed Trials – the motorcycle-only event held there each year in late August.

Brough's previous experience at Bonneville had come in 1949 when Englishman Noel Pope, one of the fastest men to ever race at Brooklands took to the salt flats with a streamlined machine, but sadly suffered a crash on his first high-speed test run.

Poper never returned with the Brough but, over 60 years later, new Brough Superior chief executive Mark Upham decided there was unfinished business and commissioned former F1 race engineer Alastair Gibson to build a special Brough machine, based on the SS100, to make a bid on the 1350-A-VG vintage class record; for rigid framed, girder-forked, un-streamlined machines, running on pump gas.

Eric Patterson (the well-respected Kempton classic show promoter), was chosen to pilot the 1150cc machine – himself already a Bonneville record holder having run 121.79mph on a Norton JAP in the pre-1956 pushrod Production Category.

Ace Cafe was there two years ago when Brough was able to celebrate in style as Patterson smashed the record, running through the traps at 124.98mph – Mark Wilsmore claiming to be the most clebrated tea boy at the event.

The team is now returning to Bonneville this year with two bikes, an SS100 Retro (a much-uprated version of Patterson's 2011 record-breaking machine) and a Pendine, built by Sam Lovegrove and based on the iconic 1927 SS100 that shares heritage and fame with Colonel T E Lawrence – Lawrence of Arabia.

There will be three riders, hoping to add more records to the Brough Superior portfolio. Patterson is joined by highly respected moto journalist (and *CBG* contributor) Alan Cathcart, another experienced man on the salt flats. The third rider is TV presenter Henry Cole.

The Ace is again backing the effort and Wilsmore says: "We're thrilled and privileged to once again be able to confirm being part of, and supporting, the Brough Superior Team heading out to break land speed records in multiple classes.

"I wanted the Ace involved because I'm an Englishman of a certain age and the Brough is the daddy of all British motorcycles. Lawrence (of Arabia) had one. It's Noel Pope. It's the 100mph barrier. It's all there.

"Mark Upham is building Brough Superiors again. How can the Ace not be involved in a project like going to Bonneville to break land speed records?"

"Mark Upham is building Brough Superiors again. How can the Ace not be involved in a project like going to Bonneville to break land speed records?"

A BROUGH TO TAKE ON BONNEVILLE

This is the stunning works Brough Superior 1150 SS100 Retro that Brit Eric Patterson is hoping to set new speed records on at Bonneville in the BUB Speed Trials on August 24-29.

Patterson is shooting for four different records, dependent on the fuel used and whether partial streamlining is fitted or not.

Alan Cathcart is the second rider on the more traditional-looking 750cc machine built by Sam Lovegrove. Cathcart's also aiming for four different class records, while TV presenter Henry Cole will also ride the 750.

Patterson's bike is called the 1150 SS100 Retro and features the latest developments of the same bike he rode in 2011 to a new record of 124.89mph in the AMA 1350-A-VG class for rigid framed, girder forked un-streamlined vintage bikes running on regular pump gasoline.

The 1087cc, 50° V-twin engine has a bore and stroke of 86mm x 94.5mm. It has twin-plug heads, 45mm inlet and 42mm exhaust valves, forged slipper pistons, 11.1 compression ration, Carillo rods.

This year's engine built by Mick Cook has 7bhp more thanks to improved cam timing and better scavenging in the sump.

Compared to the 2011 bid, this year's Bonneville project is much better prepared. The team has already been to the dyno twice with the revised bike.

A Mick Hemming six-speed replaces the original Norton three-speed 'Doll's Head' box that were used on prewar Manx Nortons and that Patterson relied on last time.

The 2013 bike should be more aerodynamically efficient. The flat section of 'seating' from the rear of the fuel tank is nothing more than a piece of upholstered carbon fibre. Then there's the tail section consisting of the seat pad plus the arty but aerodynamically functional aluminium hump. The aim being to force the rider to take more of a tucked in stance on the bike and help improve the airflow.

This year's bike sports striking aluminium bodywork – with new sidepods, handlebar fairing and seat hump. The aim is to clean up the airflow and allow the bike to cut

BROUGH CEO MARK UPHAM:
"No one has ever tried for 10 records before"

Brough Superior owner Mark Upham shares Wilsmore's British bulldog spirit and has that same in-built lust for speed. He also loves a challenge.

He's the man who brought the legendary British brand back to life by producing high-quality V-twin machines built to the same exacting standards as George Brough and, in addition to selling brand-new motorcycles that are a faithful recreation of the

original Broughs, the extrovert Upham also does everything possible to live up to George Brough's ethos of speed and reliability.

Upham chose Bonneville as a proving ground for his new Broughs and in 2011, his company's first assault on the Salt Flats, his machine established a new speed record.

"Bonneville is a battle with the elements and a place of legend," he says

emphatically. "It is also about good organisation, top class preparation, total dedication, massive team support, having good sponsors and having luck on your side. With no luck there will be no record.

"People do believe in England and its pioneers who are dedicated to achievement. George Brough chose Bonneville. We are only continuing his work."

through the air faster. But also to keep with the period look of the bike.

Total Sim, an aerodynamics company, did the (computer) simulations then Gibson had MDF sheets laser cut to produce the shape, slotted together the sheets to make the template. A local professional rolled the sheet aluminium on an English wheel to the required shape. The side pods and seat hump are made in sections (two for the pods, three for the seat), welded together and then highly polished.

This year's bike will run a new New Zealand-made ignition package. With the 2011 BTH magneto bodies bolted in place on the existing platform behind the unit. The ignition timing needs constant adjustment thanks to big fluctuation in air density caused by the intense heat. The magneto system was difficult to adjust but the 2013 system is much easier to work with and more accurate.

This year, apart from changing atmospheric conditions, the team also are running two different fuel-spec classes which means more technical changes to the bike.

ACE WORLDWIDE

THE ROAD TO
ACE CORNER

Last year's Ace Cafe-backed road trip meant 'no sleepin' till 'Bama' and saw Iron & Air magazine travelling from Brooklyn to Barber Motorsports Park for one of the most vibrant cafe racer parties ever seen outside of the UK

WORDS & PHOTOS COURTESY OF IRON & AIR

Left: The road trip starts here: The Iron & Air rig caught leaving the Big Apple.
Above: Loading up in Brooklyn and (bottom right), unloading 24 hours later in the lush green pasture of Alabama

THE ACE AT BARBER

Mark Wilsmore explains why the Ace Cafe and cafe racers are a fast growing phenomenon in the States...

How did Ace Corner come about at Barber?

The interest from the United States of America in Ace heritage, and what it represents, is quite extraordinary. There's TV shows on cafe racers there and, as such, there's a whole new generation discovering the fun to be had on two wheels. I've had the good fortune of going out to the States several times to attend events and one of the best is the Barber Vintage Festival.

What is it about Barber?

I've followed the story of Barber's growth. The guys there built this fabulous museum and race track – all specifically for bikes. They've hosted the Vintage Festival for a number of years. I went a while back and quickly realised it was the biggest and best Vintage Festival in the USA. We got into dialogue with the organisers and were invited to create an area overlooking the bulk of the circuit

– to create Ace Corner. Last year was our third year back and it's built, year on year.

How about the Iron & Air link?

We teamed up with other third parties – for example we've worked with Cafe Racer TV as well. People like them and the guys who run Iron & Air know America far better than I ever will – in terms of the burgeoning cafe racer cult.

So what was Ace Cafe contribution to the gig?

The stage – all the rock 'n roll – and the food. We even do tea but, to be fair, there's a fair bit of training that needs doing on that front. They just don't understand how to make it our way! Sweet tea is an Alabama delicacy – apparently. But they serve it cold, with lemon and no milk. It was a journey of discovery for someone who believes tea is served piping hot, with milk!

It all started when two American enthusiasts, Jason from Dime City Cycles and Mark McKee from the Ace Cafe USA, came up with the idea of Iron & Air magazine joining cafe racer enthusiasts at the Eighth Annual Barber Vintage Festival.

Jason floated the idea to Iron & Air Publisher Brett Houle and it quickly gathered pace to become reality.

Barber Motorsports Park is a modern racing facility in Alabama that hosts Indy Cars and AMA Superbike races plus major corporate events. It has a rolling topography to die for. And on the same site is the Barber Vintage Motorsports Museum, revered as one of the greatest

collections of motorcycles in the world and spanning the entire two-wheel history.

But one of the coolest events on the circuit's calendar is the motorcycle-only Barber Vintage Festival.

Barber has cordoned off an entire spectator area in one of the corners for the Ace Cafe and last year Iron & Air took a special road trip to the event.

Houle said: "The goal was to bring vintage motorcycle culture and people together in a special place carved inside the inner walls of Barber's race track, with the hope that it would springboard an annual celebration."

Houle and his team had only just finished launching the

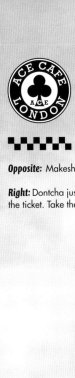

Opposite: Makeshift studio was centre point for cafe racers strutting their stuff.

Right: Dontcha just love this banner? Best seat in the house? Bikes, beers, burgers and bands? Buy the ticket. Take the ride. Who wouldn't want a piece of the action?

ACE CORNER

BARBER 2012

BEST SEAT IN THE HOUSE

BIKES, BEERS BURGERS & BANDS

CAFE RACER TV BIKE BUILDER PARK

VINTAGE MOTOS & FRIENDS EVERYWHERE

BIKE GIVEAWAY & SO MUCH MORE...

Head to Gate 4 / Turn 17
Tickets just $10

THIS IS IT SIR. *Buy the ticket,* TAKE THE RIDE.

Opposite strip:
(From top) Wilsmore lays on the British accent for the assembled American party-goers. XS650 hardtail stretches the cafe racer ethos....but the A65 on Iron & Air's booth was an absolute peach. But peaches come from Georgia, right? Well they do in Skynyrd's song! Lovely CB500 twin cafe. Another peach

Main pic.
So much to savour in the parking lot.

Bottom strip:
Left: Barber Motorsports Turn 17. Oasis for the cafe racer tribe. Right: Party over. Heading back to Brooklyn

first issue of the excellent Iron & Air magazine on-line – and was already planning the launch of the print version.

He admits now, he was scared at the prospect of over-reaching themselves but three months later, the team loaded up bikes and took a 1200-mile, 24-hour road trip from Brooklyn, New York City down to Alabama – the road to Ace Corner. As Houle said: "there was no sleepin' 'till 'Bama."

You can see from the pictures that Ace Corner at Barber attracts a huge fan base and a wide range of classic motorcycles – many in the cafe racer style that the Ace Cafe London played host to in the 1950s/60s heyday of the Ton-up boys and Rockers.

IRON & AIR MAGAZINE IS AT: www.ironandair.com
You can view the full selection of images from The Road To Ace Corner in the specially-produced Iron & Air online magazine at: http://mag.ironandair.com/i/97564

ABOUT BARBER MOTORSPORTS

Dairy magnate George Barber successfully raced cars in the 1970s.

In 1989 he started collecting and restoring them but soon turned his interest to vintage and classic bikes.

The Birmingham, Alabama native ran his own highly successful classic road racing team and collected machines for his personal museum. In 1995 he opened his collection to the public and in 2003 relocated to the purpose-built Barber Motorsports Park complex near Leeds, Alabama in 2003.

The motorcycle collection exceeds 1200 machines (600 on display at any time) and span the history of two wheels from 1902 to current days. Bikes from 20 countries represent 200 different manufacturers.

The race circuit, which hosts Indy Cars as well as AMA Superbikes, is 2.38 miles in length, features 80 feet of elevation changes and is described as one of the most beautiful tracks in North America. www.barbermuseum.org and www.barbermotorsports.com

ROCKIN'
AROUND

THE
CLOCK

"Cafes with jukeboxes were the favourites. What was important was what you rode, what you wore and the music you listened to – and the music was rock 'n' roll."
Pat Draper, first generation ton-up boy

WORDS BY PHIL MATHER

MUSIC

You take a rock, you take a beat. You take a boogie, you make it sweet. Those were the first lines of the verse in Rock-A-Beatin' Boogie, composed by Bill Haley and first recorded by The Esquire Boys in 1952 and then recorded by Bill Haley and his Comets on Decca in 1955.

Rock 'n' roll music is many things to many people. There's no denying that Bill Haley's Rock Around the Clock was a landmark track – for many people living in the UK it was the first rock 'n' roll number they ever heard. But how does it stack up against Little Richard's Tutti Frutti, Fats Domino's Blueberry Hill and Elvis Presley's Heartbreak Hotel? Are they rock 'n' roll too?

Fifty years ago the lines were easily drawn. When Elvis sang Love Me Tender it was a ballad or a love song sung by Elvis. Not like a love song by Jo Stafford or Nat King Cole because Elvis was Elvis, in the same way as Frank Sinatra was Frank Sinatra. The artist's name was the key to knowing what to expect before the stylus kissed the vinyl.

Sure Buddy Holly went a long way to stretch the rock 'n' roll envelope, from rockers like Early In The Morning to the full orchestral nine yards on It Doesn't Matter Any More, but there was never any doubt as to who was behind the microphone.

If you wanted to give any of the above a generic title it was 'popular music', although that only mattered to radio and television programme controllers and newspaper hacks. Standing in the queue at the record shop, or dropping a coin into the jukebox, you went for the name of the performer or a song title. When the band hit into At The Hop everybody got on the dance floor; when they dimmed the lights and sang Goodnight Sweetheart you held your baby close for the last dance. If anybody had the temerity to ask what it was all about, you'd say it was rock 'n' roll.

BALLS OF FIRE

There was never any live music played at the old Ace Cafe. Johnny Kidd and his Pirates may have dropped in for a late night/early morning cuppa on the way home from a gig, and Adam Faith may have swung by on his chrome-plated Triumph, but nobody shouted out, "C'mon mate, give us a tune!" Knowing the bike crowd, that wouldn't have been considered cool. In any case, there was no upright piano tucked into a corner where budding rockers could hammer out a home spun version of Great Balls Of Fire while their pals clumped around in their sea socks and flying boots. Music was available on the jukebox, if you had small change to spare, with a variety of current popular hit tunes on offer.

Since the clientele spending the money were mostly ton-up boys and girls, the selection was an even mix between cutting-edge American artists who existed far away in a land of Cadillacs and hot rod races, drive-in movies, lonesome trains and Fender guitars, and the home team recruited from the hopefuls who hung out at the 2i's coffee bar or played skiffle in village halls and at church fetes, praying desperately to be discovered by any passing impresario with a keen eye for a kid with the right 'look' and musical talent thrown in as a bonus.

Some made it and went touring around the country accompanied by a backing band of formally trained musicians, or appeared on fledgling TV shows like Oh Boy, Dig This!, Drumbeat and 6-5 Special. Nevertheless, for several years rock 'n' roll was quintessentially American – and if a lot of grown-ups had had their way it would have stayed there. Two things changed all that; in 1960, British artists finally stood on stage alongside their American counterparts and turned out to be not half bad after all, and while the establishment was forever trying to sanitise and tone things down, the genie was finally out of the bottle. Rock 'n' roll had become a big money business, and the people with the spending power were now calling the shots.

ROCKIN' THE ACE

Looking at this year's programme of events there are bike days and car days to suit any and every make and model of machine, whether it has two, three or four wheels. From its conception, the re-opened Ace was always intended to be a venue for petrolheads of all denominations, and although the bike crowd has remained firmly centre stage throughout 20 years of reunions, Brighton Burn Ups, Southend Shakedowns and Margate Meltdowns, a monthly hot rod night was established in the car park three years before the cafe was actually up and running, and subsequently four-wheeler attendance has blossomed.

As a consequence you'll get to hear anything from rockabilly, hillbilly and southern rock to soul, ska and reggae being played at the Ace on chosen nights throughout the calendar. Incidentally, I'm told what you wear is as important as what you ride or drive these days. teddy boy crepes and drapes are strictly for traditional rock 'n' roll nights. If rockabilly is your scene, guys wear blue jeans with large turnups, T-shirts and docker jackets and girls wear dungarees, and everybody has lots of tattoos. Suits and Hawaiian shirts are favoured by swing/jive males while the fairer sex, in the main, opt for cocktail dresses. Frilly jiving dresses look the business but tend to get in the way when everyone's dancing. You have to wear a Ben Sherman shirt with a three button-down collar and Levi's jeans with a minimal turnup if you're a mod male; mod girls wear BIBA and a stack of eye makeup.

There are tribute nights too, featuring a live band as well as a DJ, although for the time being these are centred on the stars like Elvis, Johnny Kidd and Billy Fury, rather than Prince Buster and Bob Marley. On a personal note, I'd be intrigued to discover what is played at the Transit Van Club meet and the Almost Famous Car Club meet – do they have an allotted genre? Do you have to bring your own handbag to the Essex Cruise Scene and do they spin Masaaki Hirao records at the Honda Culture Show?

On a less frivolous note, the Ace supports Strummerville (named after Joe Strummer of The Clash who died in 2002), a charity set up to offer support, resources and performance opportunities to fledgling musicians around the world. In the UK, some of that help has gone to the London community radio station Rinse FM which champions youth-oriented music and provides a gateway into broadcast radio and the wider music industry. It's good to know that the spirit of Sam Phillips and Alan Freed is still alive and thriving.

Below:
Vintage rock mags relive the good old days of real rock 'n' roll

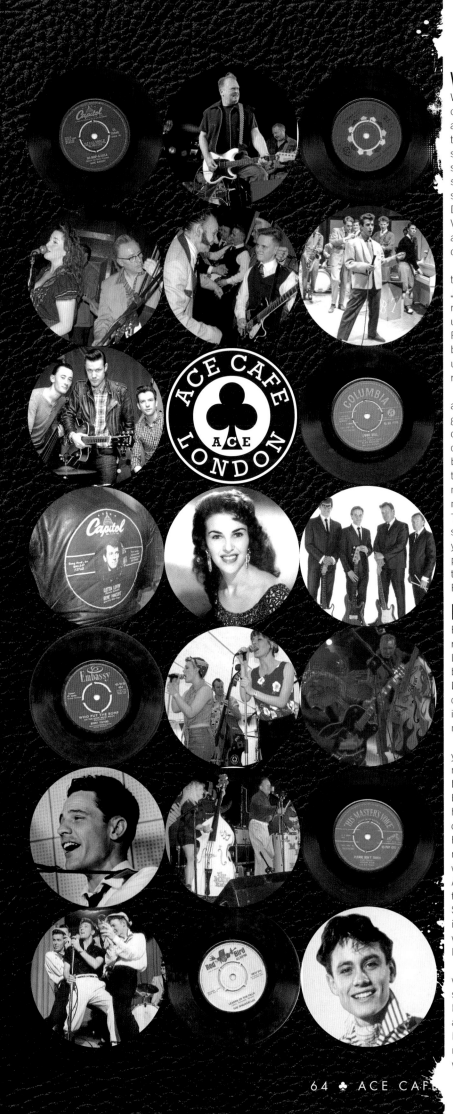

WILD AND FRANTIC

When Vee-Tone Records was asked to put together a compilation disc to celebrate the Ace's 75th anniversary, it agreed to narrow its search for suitable material down to the seven years between 1956 and 1962 – the aim 'to showcase the soundtrack of the ton-up years and subsequent rocker culture'. Out the door went the saccharine tones of Doris Day, Frank Ifield and Perry Como, so beloved of every mum and dad, and blastin' from the Dansette Conquest Auto De Luxe came the sounds of Gene Vincent, Chan Romero and Eddie Cochran. Rebellious, wild and frantic was what the man ordered, and Vee-Tone has delivered in spades.

Scanning through the list of 28 performers on the CD, the names of Roy Orbison, Billy Fury, Adam Faith and Johnny Kidd are instantly recognisable to anybody with a rock 'n' roll bone in their body, but selected tracks may be unfamiliar unless you are an ardent fan. What The Rock 'N' Roll Years does, you realise as soon as you start listening, is broaden the approach to the music of the period, not serve up the familiar chart hits that get repeated so often in retrospective collections.

That's not to say that Johnny Kidd's Please Don't Touch is a little known B-side; it was his first single release and a great number that just didn't make it on the day. On the other hand, Billy Fury's Gonna Type A Letter was a B-side, on a first release single that hedged its bets between a bouncy little number that was sure to have everybody tapping their feet and clicking their fingers on a set-piece TV music show, and the A-side Maybe Tomorrow, the kind of moody teen ballad that was to become Billy's stock-in-trade. The rhythmic clacking of a typewriter in the background sounds rather cheesy nowadays, but it's the sort of thing you have to accept on records of the period and is pardonable when you hear the inane comic voices that mar two otherwise great rockin' tracks by Peanuts Wilson and Ronnie Self, Cast Iron Arm and Ain't I'm A Dog.

DRUMBEAT

But we're here to rock 'n' roll and two of Adam Faith's records, Watch Your Step and his earlier release Ah, Poor Little Baby, will have you on the dance floor the minute the band strikes up. After appearing on the BBC's TV show Drumbeat, Adam toured the UK extensively with a line-up of British and American acts and numbers like these illustrate the hard hitting side to his stage act that packed music venues but failed to chart.

Inevitably, there are going to be numbers that remind you of other numbers, and in this case a singer that reminds you of another singer too. Vince Taylor's I Like Love sounds a lot like a marginally up-tempo version of Buddy Holly's Looking For Someone To Love, and Vince himself was an unashamed Gene Vincent clone, dressed on stage in head to toe black leather and acting mean. Falling just short of Cochran's raucous tone, but losing nothing of his drive, are singer/songwriters Ronnie Self (he wrote I'm Sorry and Sweet Nothin's for Brenda Lee) with Ain't I'm A Dog, and Chan Romero with My Little Ruby, a follow-up to his self-penned 1959 hit Hippy Hippy Shake. Self's success was sadly short-lived, but Romero's influence, and in particular Hippy Hippy Shake, spread worldwide culminating in a UK hit for The Swinging Blue Jeans.

As a representative collection of music from a period when instrumentals were seldom out of the charts, its surprising that The Rock 'N' Roll Years' only gives us one – Link Wray's Rumble. It's a slow number, strong on guitar and bass drum, with more than a hint of menace (but then I guess the title implies that). It is best heard on late night radio, the sound drifting across the outskirts of Modesto with you parked up under the stars on Highway 132, not

sheltering from the rain at a bus stop in Neasden with a flat tyre and no hope of getting a ride home.

Ever so slightly up-tempo from Rumble is Jack Scott's The Way I Walk, a polished performance with just a hint of Danny and the Juniors in the backing vocals. Scott was not a copyist, I hasten to add, developing his own individual style and writing all but one of his 19 singles record releases. Nowadays he's ranked high among the legends of rock 'n' roll, (just listen to his stormin' Leroy if you need convincing) but at the time of their release only four of his records made it into the UK charts.

Unfortunately for Sid King and the Five Strings performing their number Booger Red, they sound far too much like saintly Bill Haley and his Comets to be considered 'rebellious, wild and frantic'. Regarded for a while as 'one of the hottest rock 'n' roll acts working in Texas', it makes you realise why Roy Orbison and Buddy Holly were so keen to move to the bright lights of Memphis and Nashville. In fairness, Sid and the boys never made a serious attempt to shake their country and western roots or ditch their matching Roy Rogers stage outfits. However, they serve as a reminder that local folks didn't stop making music when the likes of Elvis and Jerry Lee shipped out, and as a consequence country rock, hillbilly and rockabilly music bubbled away under the surface, waiting to be rediscovered by a new generation.

Three tracks on this compilation illustrate this perfectly; just listen to Johnny Duncan and The Blue Grass Boys swing through Blue, Blue Heartache and Mind Your Own Business, cowboy music replete with fiddle, slap bass and brushes on a snare drum (but mercifully no yodelling), followed with a little more intensity by Johnny Burnette and the Rock 'N' Roll Trio with Tear It Up. Tear It Up was recorded in 1956; if you know some place, not too far back off the highway, a swinging joint where you can jump and shout, there's a fair bet that they'll be playing that kind of music there tonight.

Ace Cafe, The Rock 'N' Roll Years is available from the Ace Cafe (www.acecafeshop.com) or direct from Vee-Tone Records (www.veetonerecords.com).

JUST FOR KICKS
··········

Mike Sarne's cheesy 1963 Just For Kicks single, on Parlophone wasn't a hard rocking kinda' song but Ace Cafe boss Mark Wilsmore reckons the lyrics themselves pretty much sum up the cafe racer/ton-up boys' lifestyle of the 1950s/60s. You can find the song on YouTube but don't expect to be inspired by serious rock 'n' roll!

If there's one thing that I like
It's a burn up on my bike
A burn up with a bird up on my bike
Now the M1 ain't much fun
Till you try and do a ton
A burn up on my bike, that's what I like

Just for kicks, I ride all through the night
My bird hangs on in fright
When I do the ton for kicks

When my bird decides to turn up
I'm off to have a burn up
A burn up with a bird up on my bike
When I pass a little scooter
I blast him with my hooter
A burn up on my bike, that's what I like

Just for kicks, I ride all through the night
My bird hangs on in fright
When I do the ton for kicks

We meet the other ton-up boys at Fred's
Cave every night
We just drop in to see the birds and
sometimes have a bite
We spend a couple of hours just tunin'
our machines
With our black leather jackets and our
oily greasy jeans

If there's one thing that I like
It's a burn up on my bike
A burn up with a bird up on my bike
Now the M1 ain't much fun
Till you try and do a ton
A burn up on my bike, that's what I like

Just for kicks, I ride all through the night
My bird hangs on in fright
When I do the ton for kicks
(and repeat chorus)

IAN STEWART

I got my first bike at the age of 16 – in 1954. The first time I went to the Ace I think I was riding a 125cc Excelsior and my mate was on a 125 Bantam. We couldn't afford to buy a cuppa tea or egg and chips. We had no money then.

I couldn't even afford a leather jacket – just had a plastic jacket and wellies. We used to ride all year round too. I used to fall off on ice riding to work two or three times in one ride but you'd pick the bike up and think nothing of it. I can remember watching my A7 spin down the road on its crash-bar. The bikes were a lot lighter then – and there wasn't the huge amount of traffic either.

We used to have to do all our own maintenance, well I used to work on my mates' bikes too because I was the one who was on an engineering apprenticeship and the others were in the building trade and knew little about their bikes.

The Ace was a scary place anyway so we didn't dare go in. Back then there were lots of lorries and cars but only a few motorcycles. It was a dirty, stinking hole – and very cliquey. You didn't dare look anyone in the eye. There were fights, usually over girls. I can handle myself – I used to be a boxer – but I was never pushy. There were some big buggers hanging out at the Ace back then.

If you left your bike the chances are it would get nicked. I've known people nick Triumph Bonnevilles, fettle them and then race at Brands with them – and a couple of weeks later put them back where they found them!

But the attraction of the Ace for us youngsters was the motorcycles. The place had a mystique about it. But it commanded respect too.

The Busy Bee had a totally different atmosphere. I worked in Cricklewood and lived in Boreham Wood so I'd go to the Busy Bee first, meet up with some mates and then ride over to the Ace. I never saw the Ace in daylight. All the rides were in the evening – up through Wembley, Blockley Hill had no trees. And in those days there was no underpass road. You'd see the neon light of the Ace sign as you went through the series of bends approaching it. Lovely evenings…

There weren't really that many cafe racers around in the 1950s but the reason people started building them was because there were a lot of Featherbed frames lying around. There used to be a car racing class for 500 singles and all the Norton motors were snapped up for that, which meant a lot of rolling chassis going spare. The T110 motor was the best around then so people started building Tritons. Myself and my mates were scraping together the money just to keep on the road. We had nothing left to build Tritons.

Another big attraction of the old cafes was the music. We only had Radio Luxembourg then to hear the latest rock 'n' roll so we were starved of new music. We'd go to the Busy Bee or Ace and be able to listen to it on the jukebox – but also learn of new bands and records from talking to the other guys.

The other big thing for us was racing. We used to think we were fast on bikes but then we'd go to Brands and watch Geoff Duke on that Gilera four-pot Italian bike or see John Surtees and an MV and realise how fast you could go on a bike.

I was never part of the 59 Club. It didn't start as a bike club until 1962 and I was in Australia by then. I did R&D on the Blue Steel missiles and got sent out to Adelaide where they did a lot of testing. I was there from 1962-64, which meant I missed the rocker era.

When I came back I still had bikes but didn't go to the Ace so much because I was all over the place with work – spending a lot of my time at Boscombe Down. In 1967/68 I met my missus and she said no bike while the kids were young. I used to keep a Z1 Kawasaki at work…

When the Ace fired up again in the 1990s I said to my wife: "The kids are grown up, I'm back on a bike again." And it's been lovely getting back with all my old mates. I've also met a lot of people who used to do the Ace and other cafes that I never knew back in the 1960s.

I rode to the Ace for Triton Day on my A10 (when the pic, left, was taken) but I also have a 1957 Tiger 110. I'm a Triumph guy at heart. It's a typical rocker's bike – everyone had T110s or Thunderbirds. I'm 75 now but I do a few gardening jobs just to earn a little bit of petrol money to keep the bikes on the road.

I've also got a 2011 1050 Sprint for everyday riding. I just bought it after some guy in a Transit van pulled out in front of me and wrote my 2005 Sprint off. I'm with Carole Nash Insurance and I've got to say it paid out straight away.

The Ace now is hallowed ground. The beauty is that it's still the same ground, still the same building and it still has that charisma it had in the rocker era. There's still that buzz about the place. I love it.

Mark and Linda Wilsmore have done a great job in getting the Ace back on its feet. It's a wonderful place. The only difference now is that I get to see it in daylight. I don't ride at night these days and I miss those balmy nights, the smell of hot engines…

59
Made by Rockers
ROCKERS
BSA
FIFTY NINE CLUB
Thunderbird
TRIUMPH

ACE FASHION

ROCKER STYLE

It was never just the black leather jacket. It was how you dressed it up to give your own stamp of individuality that really mattered

WORDS BY GARY PINCHIN
PHOTOS BY MYKEL NICOLOAU (LEAD IMAGE), PHIL MASTERS (LEATHERS) AND MIKE COOK (B&W ARCHIVE)

1960s Highwayman
"The rumour is that this was Lemmy's (of Motörhead fame) jacket when he was in a band called The Rocking Vicars but I've not caught up with him to ask. The painting looks very early 1970s – part of that rock and roll revival."

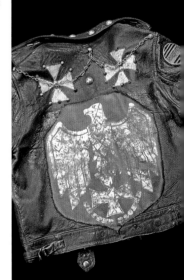

1960s unbranded
"There's no label in this jacket so I'm not sure who made it. It's got primitive studs in it. I'd say its 1960. The United Rockers patch was sold through Lewis Leathers at that time."

Black leather jacket. Turned up jeans. Engineer boots. Jet-style lid. The garb defined the 1960s Rocker. Put like that, it sounds very uniform and a style driven by function, but Rocker fashion developed into an art form as the bikers sought to express the same kind of individuality through their clothes as they did with their cafe racers.

Derek Harris owns Lewis Leathers, and is a passionate historian, not just of his own brand, but of biker fashion and culture.

"The customisation of the black leather jacket in the Rocker era is more like folk art," he says. "If you look at the American leather jackets worn by bikers, any decoration was absolutely perfect. English kids weren't deterred from decorating their jackets either – but didn't seem to worry if the decoration wasn't quite spot-on or if the logo they painted on was imperfect. I think that has a unique charm."

The Rocker style wasn't just painted bike logos and slogans like 'too fast to live, too young to die', it was studs, patches, pin badges too. The heavier the decor, the better.

"There was some talk that the studs would help you slide down the road if you came off the bike," says Derek. "And the chrome or brass finish helped you be seen at night. But function wasn't the reason. It was all about individuality and if fixing studs to your leather jacket allowed the water to seep through the surface, then so be it.

"I don't think I'd have personalised a brand new jacket in such a way but then I'm not 17. You have to remember a lot of these Rockers were just young kids."

D Lewis had made leather motorcycle jackets as far back as the 1920s, if not for casual biking, certainly for competition. The leather jacket was chosen for its wind-resistance, abrasion-resistance and water-resistance qualities but the real demand among everyday motorcyclists for leather jackets came post Second World War.

Young bikers buying ex-RAF sheepskin jackets found them great for keeping warm but they didn't offer much in the way of abrasion resistance.

Derek says: "Flying gear was popular because the kids could associate with war heroes but in 1956 Lewis produced the Bronx leather jacket catering for that market with a more direct style."

Lewis long had a leather jacket in its range that was similar to the Bronx, the style popularised by the 1953 movie The Wild One starring Marlon Brando as Johnny, the leader of a hell-raising bike club. When that launched, Lewis tweaked the old design and marketed it as its modern take on the biker jacket.

"Until then, Lewis Leathers had largely been selling Second World War surplus stock and the Bronx tested the water. There was a range of motorcycle-specific leather jackets produced on the back of that – the Highway Patrol, the Thunderbolt, and they were bought by the Ton-up boys of the 1950s.

"You have to remember, up until then the only gear would have been the longer coats that their dads wore on bikes. They didn't want to look like their dads. You can imagine the kids coming to Lewis saying 'please make something more stylish for us'. Lewis obliged with a range that set the tone for the next 20 or 30 years," says Derek.

CUSTOMISATION

It wasn't until the 1960s that Lewis provided a catalogue from which the kids could easily buy the studs, domes, patches, badges etc. to customise their jackets. Derek says: "The catalogue had ads in it that proclaimed: 'Do it yourself, we offer studs, bars etc. etc.' and 'Individualise your own clothing'. The Rocker era didn't really kick off until the 1964-66 period so the 1960 catalogue was way ahead of its time."

'The Rocker style wasn't just painted bike logos and slogans like 'too fast to live, too young to die', it was studs, patches, pin badges too. The heavier the decor, the better'

Ironically, the Rockers' obsession with decoration was nothing new. Derek's collection of ephemera includes a 1936 James Grose catalogue (a company on the Euston Road which sold a huge range of motor car and motor cycle equipment), which features a full page of handlebar mascots – including both 'death's head' and 'skull and wings' items. Derek says: "It's interesting to see that the 'devil may care' imagery goes back to a much earlier period than all of us imagine."

The Ton-up boys and subsequent Rockers certainly had a devil may care attitude – and exploited it to build their own notoriety. While there might not have been a national speed limit at the time, most citizens abided by a certain code, probably because their vehicles were not capable of excessive speeds. That all changed with the Ton-up boys and their stripped-down cafe racers. On the road they were tearaways. Off the bikes they had a image that was far removed from the very conservative mainstream fashion of the era.

PEAKED CAPS

It wasn't just their customised leather jackets. Peaked caps were part of the look too – but not derived from the Nazi uniform. "Brando wore a cap in The Wild One – as did Harley and Indian riders in the States. Caps were part of their culture and you can find them in catalogues like those from Buco – or Harley. And I think that's what kicked off the style among the Rockers. But over here the only peaked caps we had were ex-military stock, or those worn by milkmen, train drivers, garage attendants. So the kids took what they could get and customised them too," recalled Derek.

It was that way with all the early Ton-up gear. "I read about guys here wanting American-style engineers' boots. You couldn't get them so the kids bought something as close as possible and then took them to the local cobblers to have the straps added at the top and across the instep," says Derek.

Lewis had been selling ex-military surplus in the 1950s and it wasn't until 1958 that it produced the Texan boot, a short, fleece-lined engineers–styled boot with calf and instep straps. The unlined Atlantic boot followed in 1960 – as did the zip-back long boots with a cut similar to those used in horse riding. These were popular with the cafe racer boys, worn with white seaboot socks turned over the top.

LEATHER JEANS

There wasn't the intense safety campaign for riding gear back then like there is now and many of the cafe racer crowd wore jeans on their bikes, the hip brand then was made by Westcot, an English company from Cannock.

"Levis were not readily available in the UK at that time – Lewis started importing them in 1963 way before there was an official importer. The Westcot jeans were lightweight cotton compared to the heavy jeans the Americas were producing then," says Derek.

"The Westcots to have were those in black, with green stitching and zip-up back pockets. Turn-ups of course, unless you tucked your jeans into your boots! They also did blue jeans but all its products were more workwear than fashion wear at that time," Derek went on to say.

Lewis produced leather jeans too from 1957 onwards – with a silk lining that the motorcycle magazine reviews raved about for its ability to trap warm air and fend off the cold!

JET AGE MEETS CAFE RACERS

When the Ton-up/Rocker era was in full swing there was no helmet law but many bikers still wore pudding basin helmets. Yet again, it was American influence that changed the fashion this side of the Atlantic.

"The Aviakit Super Jet helmet first appeared in 1958 (Aviakit being a brand name within the Lewis company). At the time we also had the pudding basins in our catalogue and one of them was called the Skid Lid – actually being our patented name at the time.

"The Super Jet was an important addition to the catalogue for the younger rider. Up to then they had a choice of a pudding basin or the cork-style peaked helmets that the police used.

"The Super Jet was modelled on the new helmets that had been developed for the jet fighter pilots. It was a nice shape and was picked up on by British makers because it was all about new, modern, progress and speed.

"It's interesting that you can still buy jet-style crash helmets but the modern ones are a lot bigger (and have more padding) due to safety rules. Street bikers in Japan still go for the old Aviakit-style slim helmet – but that's helped since their helmet rules are not so stringent as here – and it's a lot safer riding bikes out there," says Derek.

FULL CIRCLE

In the late Sixties leather jackets began to sport fringes. In the 1970s with the infestation of glam rock on TV came coloured leathers; the track influence brought racing stripes, mandarin collars, quilted padding.

But we're back to black in 2013. Derek says: "When I took over Lewis Leathers in 1991/92 I reintroduced the classic styles and only did black jackets for 10 years. In 2001/2002 we introduced mid-blue and then navy but were very conservative. Now we do the full spectrum of colours with France and the Far East both being popular markets for coloured leathers. I don't know why that is. But British riders demand almost exclusively black leathers – like 99% of them."

Lewis Leathers, like bike fashion, has worked its way full circle since the 1960s. Back in vogue are cafe racers – as is the black leather jacket. You could argue neither really went away. It's just that there's a lot more focus on the cafe race culture right now.

■■■■■■■■■■■■■■■■■■■■■■■■■■■■■■■■■■■■

1960S BRONX

"This was Father Graham's jacket. It's got a scuba-diving patch above the 59 club patch. That's because Father Graham introduced a scuba diving club. It's a classic twin-track Bronx jacket."

1960s Bronx
"It's a classic 1960s Bronx jacket with a Lewis Leathers label. All the badges are of 1960s vintage. It's a great snapshot of the period."

1960s Highwayman Florida
"This would have cost £15-7s-6d at the time and features a collection of rare Aviakit badges from the mid-1960s and a 59 Club patch. The story is that this belongs to a group of kids who hung out at a Red Lion pub. They adopted the pub logo as their 'club' emblem and incorporated the 59 Club badge in the centre."

1960s origin uncertain
"I found this on eBay. It was possibly owned by a female – Emily is painted on it. There's no label, but the stitching looks typical Lewis Leathers. It's very similar in style to jackets used in the 1969 movie 'The Battle of Britain'. It was funny seeing all the Luftwaffe pilots in Lewis Leathers."

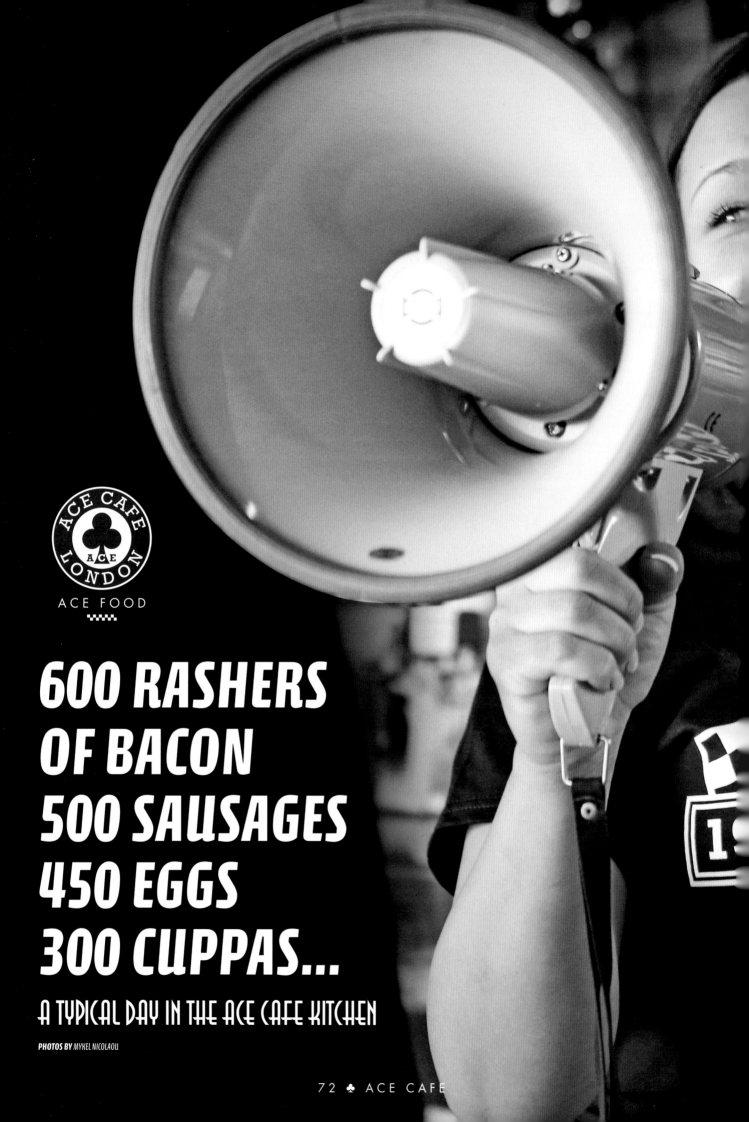

ACE FOOD

600 RASHERS OF BACON
500 SAUSAGES
450 EGGS
300 CUPPAS...

A TYPICAL DAY IN THE ACE CAFE KITCHEN

PHOTOS BY *MYKEL NICOLAOU*

Above:
Ace fish and chips. British staple.
Another great reason for a ride
to the cafe.

THE young waitress steps forward, steaming hot plate of cheesy, chilli chips in one hand, loud hailer in the other. "Number 236", she announces over the din of the packed cafe.

Amid the mayhem, someone waves a hand to catch her eye, and off she rushes to despatch the meal to an expectant customer.

It gets hugely busy at the Ace, especially during the special Sunday bike days, when people spill out into the car park as the cafe fills up.

When you order food, you are given a ticket with a number on it. The rule is, stay in the cafe until your food is ready. Service at the Ace is top notch. You never sit waiting for long – even at the busiest times.

The Ace might be the place where petrolheads hang out, but its core business, ever since 1938, has been built on selling fast food.

Back in the early days, the term 'fast food' hadn't been invented (according to Wikipedia, it first found its way into a Merriam-Webster dictionary in 1951) but the Ace was a transport cafe nonetheless, selling typical greasy spoon-style fayre.

These days, while the cafe has retained it's sparse utility furnishings, and in some ways remains a stopping off point for those who earn their business driving vans and lorries, the menu is as varied as the type of people frequenting the place.

The Ace opens at 7am and does a roaring trade in breakfasts. It never seems to calm from there… the kitchen closes at 10pm and the Ace locks its doors at 11pm. In between time, the place is a hive of activity.

Marek Bartoska is one of five duty managers at the Ace, but he's flexible. Sometimes he's on kitchen manager duty – he spent years working as a head chef in previous

Above: Happy in their work. It's always busy in the galley kitchen of the Ace Cafe

employment – other times he's the maintenance manager. It all depends on the demands of the day.

He says: "In the mornings and lunchtimes we get passing trade from drivers in the area, then there are the people who work nearby, and even locals drop in for breakfast. In the evenings its mainly the bikers or car enthusiasts – the petrolheads.

"We can do anything between 200 to 600 meals a day, depending on what's going on here. Normally there are three people serving and three cooking, but for events when we know we are going to be busy we have five or six on both sides."

No wonder the complete Ace staff rosters number more than 20 people during the 'season', which runs from March to October (trade tends to drop away in the winter months – as you might expect).

Marek reckons that on average Ace customers consume about 600 rashers of bacon, 500 sausages, 450 eggs, up to 200 burgers and over 300 cups of tea each day (and operations manager George Tsuchnikas jokes that Mark Wilsmore drinks half of them!) each day. But the menu offers much more, including: ribs, pies, curries, gammon steaks, fish 'n' chips, and scampi. There are eight breakfast options, including a healthy oat porridge and Manx kippers (how Isle of Man TT can you get?), 12 main meals, plus a further six

'The Ace opens at 7am and does a roaring trade in breakfasts. It never seems to calm from there... the kitchen closes at 10pm and the Ace locks its doors at 11pm. In between time, the place is a hive of activity'

ACE CAFE ♣ 75

different types of Ace Burger Specials and five different Ace Sausage Specials.

However it's the typical staples that the Ace customers seem to go for.

Marek adds: "I'd say the two most popular things on the menu are the full English and the burgers.

"I've a lot of experience in the food industry and previously worked as a chef, but the thing I like about the Ace is that things like the sausages and burgers are made by a local butcher to our recipe. It is quality food and not straight from the freezer cabinet as some people might expect."

Like any other cafe, there are specials on offer, but the basic menu varies only occasionally. "I've been here four years and in that time the menu has changed twice," says Marek. "It's flexible and if people want things added then that's possible, and the things that aren't popular get deleted. It's normal (for any cafe). But I think the Ace has been going long enough and has the experience to understand what its customers like, so maybe that's why this current version of the menu has been the same for two years."

'Things like the sausages and burgers are made by a local butcher to our recipe. It is quality food and not straight from the freezer cabinet as some people might expect'

Above:
Duty manager Marek devides his daily duties between bar sales, kitchen management and maintenance work

Opposite:
Kebabs and Merch at the Ace

ACE VET

DICK BENNETT

I went to the Ace in 1968/69 – I was there for the final year of the original cafe. I was in the 59 Club and one night someone said: 'let's go for a run up to the Ace'. It was the usual gathering; a few cafe racers and lots of Matchless singles. There were never many cafe racers because people couldn't afford things like that back then.

You'd get the occasional nice Triton – but it was a minority, not the hundreds of bikes that the myth would have you believe. There were lots of 250 A-jays, M20 BSAs. People used their bikes for everyday transport back then – and you rode in all weathers. Even the big twins were a bit ratty and well used.

I had a 250cc CB72 Honda, which I bought for £30 and knocked about on.

I started my apprenticeship at Paddington Technical College and the 59 Club was in Paddington at that time too. I wasn't even old enough to ride a bike at the time but one night some lads said they were off to the 59 Club and I tagged along.

I just kept going to the club once I'd bought my Honda as a 16-year-old. I was on five quid a week as an apprentice.

In those days people used to a do a round robin kind of ride. There would be some coming from the Ace to the 59. Chelsea Bridge is eight miles from the Ace so we'd ride down there. And there was the Busy Bee just up the road. Then there was the Cellar Cafe at Windsor, which if you had a reliable enough bike, you might go to. One of the lads used to live on the other side of London and used to ride down to Johnsons near Brands Hatch.

The thing was that it was rare to just hang out all night at the Ace. You did sometimes but more often than not, you'd ride there, meet up with some mates, stay for maybe an hour, have a cuppa and then, more often than not, you'd go for a ride.

Even back in the 1960s you weren't allowed in the pubs in your bike gear so you went places where you were allowed in and that's why everyone tended to go to the transport cafes.

I'd be out every night on my bike – well, every night I could until I ran out of money for petrol. But Thursday night you'd be struggling for cash. Then Friday you'd get paid again. The whole lifestyle was finance driven. It's such a different world now.

In the old days of the 59 Club, you'd be accepted on any bike (as now). A lot of people rode things like Bantams and James. It certainly wasn't a case of fifty-odd Bonnevilles roaring down Chelsea Bridge.

When the Ace shut, Chalky White's opened just down the road from the Ace and we went there for a while. But it developed a bit of a, what you would now call, backpatch atmosphere so we gradually drifted away.

Back then we lived through times when a lot of people relied on two-wheel transport. The 59 Club was going well by then.

It started, as you'll probably be aware, from the Ace in the early 1960s. Father Bill Shergold used to ride his 650 Triumph around his parish and used to come to the Ace. I remember hearing how, the first time he went to the Ace, he rode up and down outside for four or five times before having the courage to go in to the cafe.

There was a lot of bad press about the Ton-up lads at the time and he organised a blessing of the bikes at his church. It was something all the newspapers got hold of.

At that time, there was a youth club at his church called The 59 Club and by 1962 the bikes had taken over the youth club and went from strength to strength.

Because of the link with the Ace, we (The 59 Club) have always kept in touch with Mark (Wilsmore) and have always had a good relationship with the Ace.

We're a charity, we're volunteers. He's commercial. But the ethos for both has always been the same. It's all about having fun with bikes and having somewhere to go.

The 59 Club was, and still is, a tea/coffee bar, just like the Ace. You ride in, have a tea, chat bikes and then go for a ride. There were no rules then and there are no rules now. Nothing was ever formalised although we used to have a regular run to Chelsea Bridge once the Club closed at 10.30pm. That replaced the Ace for us.

These days I've got an M20 BSA, an F4 MV Agusta and this BMW cafe racer. It's based on a 1979 R80 and I bought it as a bit of a rat bike built from 1960s and 70s classic bits.

ACE CAFE LONDON

ACE RACING

GO RACE
TASTE THE ACE

Having teamed up with T3 Racing, the
Ace Cafe is being featured at major road
racing events this year – at the TT and in
the British Supersport series held at
British Superbike meetings

WORDS BY PHIL MATHER
PHOTOS BY STEPHEN DAVISON (TT), TIM KEETON (BSS)

acer road, to road racer. The Ace is steeped within a history of street racing rockers. The Sixties. When the ton-up boys used to race along the North Circular to and from the cafe. In the Sixties the ton-up boys used to happily race each other on the open roads. But that was a time before blanket speed limits. These days if you really want to let rip, then it's only the racetrack that lets you really satisfy the need for speed.

And that's why the Ace has teamed up with T3 Racing. The two go back some. In 2008 the Ace commissioned Tony Scott, whose T3 Racing company specialises in things Triumph, to build a very special Ace 904S Thruxton Special cafe racer (see page 20).

So when the Ace decided to branch out and get involved with road racing, who better to form an alliance with than T3 Racing – and Triumph?

The plan was to field an Ace Cafe-liveried T3 Racing Triumph Daytona 675R in British Supersport for rider 2012 Triumph Triple Challenge title-holder Rob Guiver – and then run the bike at the Isle of Man, initially with TT specialist

Steve Mercer. But when he broke his scaphoid just prior to the event, another TT hero, Aussie David Johnson was drafted in.

Tony Scott, who also runs the Triumph Triple Challenge race series – a support series held at BSB rounds – as well as owning T3 Racing, said: "The Ace Cafe is an iconic brand with a clear link to Triumph Motorcycles in its history.

"We already knew the Ace well through our cooperation on the 904S and they are good people to work with, so when the opportunity presented itself to join with them we needed no persuasion.

"We have been racing at BSB in 600cc Stocksport and Supersport 600 for the past two years now and have never failed to finish in the top two of our chosen championship. I feel confident that this alliance will bring a fresh team and a great vibe to the BSB paddock."

Rob Guiver is mid-term with his rookie Supersport campaign and is a consistent top three finisher in the Cup (privateers) competition that runs concurrent with the overall championship.

"We have been racing at BSB in 600cc Stocksport and Supersport 600 for the past two years now and have never failed to finish in the top two of our chosen championship. I feel confident that this alliance will bring a fresh team and a great vibe to the BSB paddock"

WILSMORE ON RACING

Ace Cafe boss Mark Wilsmore loves racing and reveals the connection between the cafe, T3 Racing, Triumph's racing effort – and the TT...

Why has the Ace Cafe become involved in racing?
It's a kind of a flag-waving thing for us. Triumph only ever did racing in fits and starts – but when it did, it was always hugely successful. And for the Ace to now become part of the Triumph racing heritage today is brilliant. Racing's brilliant. It's what it's all about. I am quite sure the, 'win on Sunday, sell on Monday' element to racing still applies too. Not just in selling bikes. In our case it'll be selling eggs and bacon!

Is this a long-term thing?
The link with the T3 Racing project is a big learning curve for us. We're committed to it and we intend to grow it. I want us to be as distinct in racing as the livery is for Milwaukee Yamaha or Repsol Honda. And it's not just about stickers on bikes. It's about awareness. The public don't go racing like they did. They watch it on television. The TT is now mainstream television.

How important was it to be linked to a team running a British bike?
Totally. Over the years, Triumph racing privateers have come and gone to the TT. ValMoto did it with Bruce Anstey and were successful. And they won in British Supersport with the late Craig Jones. Our involvement fits with Triumph going racing. It's a natural thing for us to do. If we can go racing with the Ace, as a part of delivering speed, then maybe we can encourage other people to take to the track.

You first got involved with T3 Racing and British Supersport. And now you've done the TT together. Was that always the plan?
Yes, because the TT is the ultimate form of racing. Of course, I appreciate what it takes to do MotoGP, WSB and BSB, but the TT is special. And it's the natural progression from the North Circular! The involvement from BSB gave us the means to be at the TT and I hope we can grow our involvement with road racing. Our ability to do things is how to deal with those occasions. There's loads more we can do (outside events). But arguably the TT is the greatest race there is and we want to be part of it.

TONY SCOTT ON THE ACE LINK

We kicked off a relationship with the Ace Cafe through the Thruxton project bike so it was a natural progression for the Ace to come to BSB, through an involvement in the Triumph Triple Challenge. The winner of the series gets a ride in British Supersport the following year (hence Guiver being on the Ace liveried bike in British Supersport). And running that bike in Ace livery gives the Ace real presence.

We've run the Triumph Triple Challenge for seven years – four years as a club series, the past three with BSB – and there's an agreement with BSB and Triumph for a further three years.

The Ace became involved with the Triple Challenge at the start of this year, with the idea to also create an Ace Cafe within the BSB paddock. People can buy a tickets to enjoy hospitality with the Ace.

Our role is to attract a new audience to the Ace by opening the brand to a whole new audience and judging from the feedback we had at the TT, it's working well. There was a real buzz about the Ace Cafe London while we were at the TT.

It's an iconic brand and the feedback we got in the Island was phenomenal.

We set the Ace Cafe (merchandise stall) up next to the grandstand and in the race paddock we had the race truck. We had guys turning up at our garage from all over Europe, sporting Ace logos on their helmets. Some Belgian guys we met said they'd never visited the Ace but it was great to get a taste of it in the Island.

The team also enjoyed a fantastic TT debut in late May/early June with Johnson (better known in racing circles as DJ) finishing 13th in both of the Supersport races, to earn two coveted silver replicas.

Tony Scott said: "DJ put in a tremendous performance with our Daytona 675 Ace Cafe Racer. Even though we had to run a stock engine, we were still the fastest Triumph on track recording 153mph as he came down the start-finish straight in race two.

"We had taken three engines to the TT. We blew the first supersport engine. It was the first time we've ever blown an engine. It only had eight miles on it. We daren't risk the second supersport engine we had because we needed it for short circuits so I made an executive decision to run a superstock engine. It was a good call because it showed how strong the stock engine actually is. We did a 121mph lap and got a much better result with it than we ever expected."

In race one after four laps of the 37.73-mile Mountain Course, the bike ran out of fuel just as DJ crossed the line so extra capacity was added to the fuel tank for race two.

He made it across the line with enough fuel to celebrate with a burnout on the pit access lane right outside the Ace Cafe T3 Racing Team hospitality truck.

DJ's first outing produced a race average of 119.479mph. In race two he clocked an even better race average of 120.150mph.

T3 Racing's team manager Dave Harris said: "It's been two amazing performances since he's basically been riding a Triumph Triple Challenge bike (i.e. stock engine). The only real difference is that we fitted new suspension to suit the TT course! I daren't tell him that (he was running a stock motor) because he might not have done what he did if he'd known!"

Tony Scot was delighted by the performance and added: "We finished top Triumph and won two silver replicas at our debut IoM TT. Are we proud!"

The Ace Cafe T3 Racing Team will continue to race in the Motorpoint British Supersport Championship, with Rob Guiver aboard the T3 Racing-tuned and prepared, black and white liveried, Triumph 675R Daytona.

IT'S NOT JUST WHERE YOU'RE FROM. IT'S WHERE YOU'RE GOING.

THRUXTON 900

It's true. No other bike comes with the same iconic British heritage. But for decades we've been focussed on something else as well. A relentless approach to engineering that gives our bikes a look, sound and ride like no other. And we'll never stop. We will always strive to create the perfect motorcycles, for that perfect ride. Can anyone ever get there? Who knows. But then, it's all about the journey.

triumphmotorcycles.co.uk

CLASSIC 60'S BRITISH CINEMA

The Leather Boys

RITA TUSHINGHAM
DUDLEY SUTTON
COLIN CAMPBELL

PG

DVD
VIDEO ™

ACE FILM

THE REAL STORY OF
THE LEATHER BOYS

It might have stood the test of time as a motorcycle movie. But, as so often is the case, the reality is quite different to the myth

WORDS BY PHIL MATHER

Cult status in the movies is something we're all familiar with. But while James Bond and Star Wars tick all the right boxes for millions of fans worldwide, a film doesn't have to be a great box office success, doesn't have to have a cast of screen legends, doesn't have to have a great script, to attract a cult following. In fact, in many ways all these things can work against it.

Some would argue that in its truest form a cult movie is one that is generally forgotten, endeared to only a few zealots, lost in the labyrinth of minority interest sub-cultures that pervade society. It holds an attraction for a special few, encapsulating a certain time, a certain place, raising a smile or reviving a memory, bringing home a pertinent truth that few can share or understand.

The fact that the film in question, The Leather Boys, engenders allegiance from two distinct social groups makes it unusual. Then again, there are those who would smudge the division between motorcycle cult film and gay interest cinema. In a 21st century western world that may not be so much of an issue, but in the UK in the early Sixties, when the film was released, teenagers struggled for recognition and homosexuality was illegal. Adults felt they had a duty to protect youth from dressing inappropriately, listening to 'jungle beat music', sex, and riding motorcycles. Most grown-ups had a very narrow outlook on life – as one risqué joke famously quotes a woman as saying, "I didn't know what a homosexual was till I met my husband!"

If you've only ever flicked through clips from the film on the internet, linked with ton-up boys and rocker reunions, burn-ups and pounding guitar instrumentals, all this may seem a little confusing. But the story of The Leather Boys didn't start with a bunch of happy-go-lucky young chaps slapping each other on the backs and exchanging light-hearted banter about the performance of this bike or that, all the while drinking tea and furiously polishing away imaginary specks of road dirt and grime from petrol tanks and back mudguards with an oily rag. It didn't even start at the Ace Cafe. The action, such as it was, all happened far, far away from the North Circular Road.

IN THE BEGINNING

Gillian Freeman was an up-and-coming author when her publisher, Anthony Blond, commissioned her to write a story about a 'Romeo and Romeo in the south London suburbs'. For Blond, who was bisexual, it was a poke at society that stubbornly refused to acknowledge that one man could love another and show it in a physical way. For Freeman it was an opportunity to bolster her status in the avant garde world of young writers.

The resulting novel, published in 1961, describes the brief relationship between one young man, Dick, estranged from his parents and living with his recently widowed grandmother, and another, Reggie, trapped in a loveless marriage to a vacuous young trollop named Dot. At night, while Reggie rides his motorcycle to the local street corner cafe to hang out with the bike crowd, Dot seeks comfort in their bed with other men.

Superficially, the action centres around the escalating lawlessness perpetrated by the lads at the cafe, most of whom ride motorcycles. They wear leather gear, partly, so we're told, because it's a kind of uniform that gives them a feeling of power and partly 'because the girls like it'. So far, so good – but if you're already feeling just a teeny bit nervous, think Gene Vincent and Alvin Stardust.

Worryingly, however, there are men who come down to the cafe in cars. They also wear leather gear, and some of the lads 'go off' with them to earn a bob or two. Could be innocent enough I suppose, but then these blokes are referred to as 'kinky' or 'the leather johnnies' so don't say you haven't been warned. Further cause for concern is the self-styled leader of the gang, Les, who wears all the clobber, including a crash helmet, but bombs around in a ratty old car 'with drawings and objects all over it'. That's what comes of parking in Peckham.

A little later we are told that Les's car has 'yellow doors and a false red chimney pot'. Clearly Les is a bit of a nutter and this is Gillian's way of letting the reader know. Either that, or he aspires to running a burger van but hasn't got the readies to afford one yet.

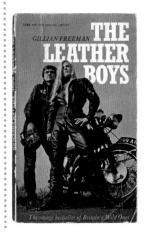

Dick meets Reggie at the cafe one night and tags along when the gang go to a dance in a church hall which they 'liven up' by smashing chairs, crockery and the record player and pouring a bottle of milk over the vicar. Les then gets them to wreck the home of the caretaker at his old school because the bloke got him into trouble for breaking windows. Amid all this puerile violence, Dick finds himself becoming attracted to Reggie – and Reggie finds he has a mate who he'd rather spend time with than with Dot.

So far the only motorcycle action has been when Reggie takes Dick over to Primrose Hill on the edge of Regent's Park in London late one night for a ride, but now they go to Southend for the day to avoid getting involved in another of Les's plans and to get Reggie out of having to have to attend the ritual Sunday lunch with Dot's mother. Dick clearly gets a big kick out of riding on the back of Reggie's bike and isn't keen when they spend some time on the beach with two girls. Later, after they've dumped the girls, Dick buys Reggie an ice cream and they're now clearly the best of pals. Then, that night, instead of going home to his wife, Reggie stays with Dick and things between the two of them get serious.

The story doesn't end there but the conclusion, either because Freeman feels she's gone about as far as she dare with the 'Romeo and Romeo' bit, or because she isn't sure just what two gay blokes would get up to next, is both tragic and inconclusive. Having decided to run away to sea together, Dick and Reggie attempt a burglary to raise some funds but come away empty handed. They get cornered by Les's gang and are badly beaten for stepping out of line and doing a job on their own, so badly that Reggie dies.

The police round the gang up and they all get sent to prison – Les, in particular, is identified as Reggie's killer by the tiger's head painted on the back of his jacket. Dick, having recovered from his injuries, gets let off and leaves the courthouse on Reggie's bike. At some traffic lights another bike, 'new and powerful', pulls up alongside, its young rider clad head to toe in immaculate leather. The lights change and they drag off into the sunset.

AND NOW THE FILM

If you've seen the film you may have noticed a few similarities, but you won't have recognised the plot. In 1961, amid all the hype and bad publicity surrounding the ton-up crowd on the North Circular, any story with a name like The Leather Boys must have seemed like too good a band wagon not to jump onto – well, at least the title worked.

Take a few well-worn cinematic scenarios of the period – kitchen sink dramatics enacted between warring, stereotypical working class family elements almost to the point of farce, spats between a newly wed couple (he expects a meal on the table when he comes home from work and a clean shirt to wear, she wants to go to the cinema with her mates and spend time at the hairdressers), a comic character or two and a few tasteless jokes – then add some tearaways on motorbikes in the background, and you've got yourself a winner.

At least that seems to have been the thinking at Merton Park Studios when Gillian Freeman was asked to come up with a screenplay more in keeping with its stock-in-trade B-movie productions. And since it wasn't in the business of offending anybody in authority, could she soft peddle the homosexual bit?

Consequently, while Dot remains unremittingly promiscuous, husband Reggie is simply a naive dupe who needs to do some growing up. As for the third character in this little menage, he's called Pete. Pete's an ex-merchant seaman who rides a big Norton and has a tiger's head painted on the back of his leather jacket.

Pete's a bit of a loner, a bit of a lad, a bit of a stirrer where Dot and Reggie are concerned, but he's not in the least bit psychopathic. There's no gang either, no violence and no brushes with the law. And there's certainly no sex, hetro or otherwise. Thinking about it, Freeman could quite easily have done her job with a pair of scissors and a pot of glue.

Considered in the context of British cinema of the period, the result is uninspiring. It's as though Rita Tushingham, who had the star role as Dot, was taking time out between her cinematic debut in A Taste of Honey and her next big picture Doctor Zhivago, honing her method acting while working with a thin script.

Compared to Whistle Down the Wind and The Innocents, The Leather Boys is definitely second rate. It took the stature of performers like Dirk Bogarde and Sylvia Syms to tackle the subject of homosexuality full-on in Victim, and despite a valiant effort by Dudley Sutton, playing the part of Pete with a commendable degree of sensitivity (he'd obviously read the book), you could quite easily believe his character was just a sensitive boy who hadn't met the right girl yet.

So does the film have any saving graces, and why, if it isn't a motorcycle movie, has it stayed on the biker radar for so long? The answer to both these questions lies in the footage shot at the Ace Cafe and on a motorcycle endurance run the lads stage to Edinburgh and back.

The choice of cafe location obviously stems from the media attention of the time – the Ace being something more than humble corner caff by day, coffee bar by night. It was, for a time, the ton-up boys' mecca, and the more publicity it received, the more motorcyclists flocked to it. When anybody wants to see what the Ace was like at its height of popularity, they only have to watch the film.

As for the run, Merton Park Studios was only a small operation working with a small budget. It co-opted Ace regulars for the riding shots and although a handful did travel up to Edinburgh, mostly with their bikes in a removal van, the location shots were staged at Frensham Pond on the A287 in Surrey (the pull-in with the tea wagon) and at the Devil's Punchbowl near Hindhead (the Golden Hind Cafe where Dot and Reggie dance to a record on the jukebox). For added realism, a group of bikes race past the A702/A766 signpost to Edinburgh (both roads lead to a single destination) which is about 12 miles outside the city, and in the next shot the riders wind up the hill to the castle.

On the soundtrack the bikes sound like proper bikes and on the night ride back to London (when one guy's Ariel Arrow suffers a 'partial seizure' – nice touch of authenticity) it snows. That's proper motorcycling!

'In 1961, amid all the hype and bad publicity surrounding the ton-up crowd on the North Circular, any story with a name like The Leather Boys must have seemed like too good a band wagon not to jump onto'

ERIC PATTERSON

Ah, the Ace Cafe. It was always a bumpy, battered old car park. Full of puddles. I lived in Windsor when I used to ride over here in the 1960s. It's about 25 miles away and it was all flat out. Invariably we'd end up with a couple of blown-up bikes on the way among our gang.

We used to hang out at the Cellar cafe in Windsor. I reckon on a good night there'd be about 60 of us. We'd ride over to Camberley to the Manor cafe. There was a four mile straight like an old airfield that way. Then there was the ride to the Ace. There'd be about 25-30 bikes.

I started riding bikes at the age of 14 – and was 16 and on the road in 1962.

I had a Tiger 110 for a while then, around 1967/68, I got a BSA Super Rocket. Bought it for £79 at Pride and Sharks as we called it (the official shop name was Pride and Clarke Ltd, on Stockwell Road, London. They held a huge range of stock and took big ads in the weekly bike press). It was £79 and 10 shillings to be exact. I ended up putting a rod through the cases and chucked that in the back of the shed and bought a BSA Shooting Star. Rebuilt the Rocket later.

The Viscount I've ridden over here today was around back then and may well have been a bike ridden to the Ace. It was bought brand new off Tom Somerton by Pete Ross in 1959. Somerton had ridden a racing Norvin built by Peter Darvill and decided to build similar road-going bikes. The plan didn't work because he couldn't get enough donor engines – but this one has a blue-printed Black Shadow engine and is absolutely beautiful to ride.

When we used to come to the Ace, a typical night out was a blast over here, grab a bite to eat and a drink, then blast on to the Busy Bee.

The Ace food was usually bacon, eggs and chips. Always chips. I'm not allowed any now. I've dieted down to 12

stone to ride at Bonneville on the works Brough Superior. We got a new world record there in the BUB Speed Trials 2011 with the Brough. Now we're going back again and trying for several different records (all with the same V-twin bike based on streamlining and fuel used). I've had an apple for lunch today. I'd love a plate of chips right now!

I used to drink tea in summer here – and hot chocolate in winter. Yeah, we used to ride all year round. We didn't care about the wet and cold – you don't when you're young do you?

The most time we'd spend at the Ace was a couple of hours. We'd meet up with some lads from London we'd not normally see, have a chat and then get back on the bikes. That's all we wanted to do really, ride bikes. We thought nothing of taking a blast down to Brighton from the Ace on a Sunday.

The whole mods and rockers thing was blown out of all proportion. I know there were some famous rucks (particularly at the southern coastal resorts) but generally we all got on. I used to know a lot of the lads and even used to have a go on their scooters. Mind you, I'd tell them what bloody horrible things I thought they were.

I still see some of the old mods – and rockers for that matter. A lot of them say they are too old to ride now. Age doesn't stop me. It's all a state of mind isn't it?

Couple of my old mates still ride. Kev Joshing's got a Gold Star he's still gets out and about on it and Dave O'Rourke – he's still riding the V-twin JAP that Dave Degens built him.

Ah, we had some good times here – still do. But I remember back then, I had long hair right down my back. We used to sit on the wall (by the main road) and eye up all the birds. There was a lot of girls riding bikes back then – a lot more than you see now. Tasty looking birds they were too!

'We'd meet up with some lads from London we'd not normally see, have a chat and then get back on the bikes. That's all we wanted to do really, ride bikes. We thought nothing of taking a blast down to Brighton from the Ace on a Sunday'

TOP GEAR

It's not just bikes. The four-wheel fraternity
play a big part in the success of the Ace

PHOTOS COURTESY OF THE ACE

ACE FOUR WHEELS

The Ace Cafe might have earned notoriety through bikes in the heydays of the 1950s Ton-Up Boys and the 60s Rockers, but these days, cars play a big role in the weekly programme of events.

Hot Rods and numerous specialist car clubs enjoy their own respective regular meetings, but then there are the big events that really draw the numbers and, as Mark Wilsmore points out: "We have far more car meets than bikes – double, in fact. There are 20 car meets per month, compared to 10 for bikes.

"We have anything from classics to Hot Rods, to modern drift cars. There's also modern car clubs. They're all petrolheads.

"What we don't have any more are one-make nights – like Ford nights or all-Japanese car nights. They got so big that we used to bring the North Circular to a standstill.

"It means the scene has fragmented down to Ford Escort RS nights or Evo Specials, but the bottom line is that car nights account for a huge part of the Ace Cafe scene."

Wilsmore: 'We have anything from classics to Hot Rods, to modern drift cars. They're all petrolheads'

ACE MERCH!

No matter what the motorcycle event, no matter where in the world you might be, chances are you'll spot the Ace Cafe logo on a bike, helmet, T-shirt or jacket. The brand is global but the one stop shop to get Ace merch is the Ace Cafe. You can buy from the online Ace store, but the best way is to get along to the Ace Cafe, sample some of the hospitality and do your shopping in the old fashioned way. Beware though, what we've shown on these pages is just a token sample of the huge range on offer. Retail therapy at the Ace could leave you with a big hole in your wallet...

PINS

The choice of badges is large. Ace lists 17 in its catalogue and they range from straight forward Ace Cafe to special event badges.

MUGS

Ace offer several different liveried mugs – chequered flag, Rockers, or StoMoCo (Stonebridge Motor Company). In black or white. Each is priced £4.90. There's also a 10oz mug and a complete range of crockery, including a full dinner service.

WALLETS

There's three leather wallets in the catalogue, each of them comes with a chain to secure it to your jeans. There's also two leather pouches in the catalogue.

STICKERS

Another huge choice, not just of styles, but also sizes. Most styles come in mini, small, medium or large. So you can sticker your bike, car, garage wall – or home!

BELTS

Ace offer two top quality black webbing belts with adjustable snap-fastening buckles with either Ace Cafe London or Rockers logos.

TOPS

There's two different hoodies: Speed Thrills and Rockers Piston (£39 each) plus an Ace hoodie sweatshirt (£44.95) – or a plain Ace sweatshirt (ie: no hood – £35). All come in five different sizes (S, M, L, XL, XXL).

BOOKS

The bookstand at the Ace has something for everyone with subject matter ranging from bikes to cars, to music, to fashion and tattoo art. Outstanding is Pride and Glory, The Art of the Rockers' Jacket by Horst A. Friedrichs (price: £85). A word of warning though, it's a weighty tome and not the sort of thing you'll be sticking up the front of your leather jacket to ride home with. Freidrichs' earlier book, Or Glory, 21st Century Rockers is also exceptional (price £14.99). But if it's the history of the Ace you want to learn about then you absolutely need the brilliant Ace Times, Speed Thrills and Tea Spills, a Cafe and a Culture by Mick Duckworth (price £29.95) or the paperback Ace Cafe, Then and Now (price £14.95).

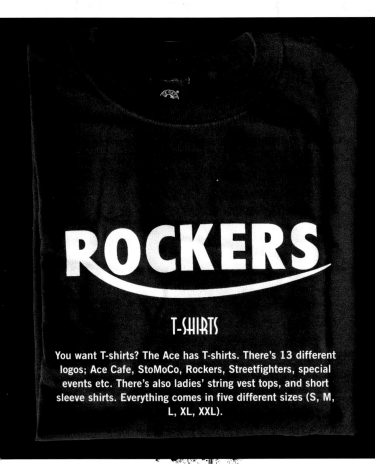

ROCKERS

T-SHIRTS

You want T-shirts? The Ace has T-shirts. There's 13 different logos; Ace Cafe, StoMoCo, Rockers, Streetfighters, special events etc. There's also ladies' string vest tops, and short sleeve shirts. Everything comes in five different sizes (S, M, L, XL, XXL).

LEATHER JACKETS

Very much a limited edition collection, there are three options of Ace Cafe leather jacket: Rocker, Ace and Ace Cafe Racer – all made by Lewis Leathers. Each is made to order and each style is priced the same; £625 plus postage and packing. Ace also offers an RAF-style Flying Jacket for £571 plus postage and packing. Sizes are 36in-44in and like the leather jackets, these are made to order.

HATS

Off your bike you'll need a beanie or hat. Ace does several styles. They also sell a range of bandanas and scarfs, including the traditional rocker's white silk scarf. There's a more up to date version of the old bikers' scarf, known as the 'neckwarmer' and Ace has a good range of them, both plain and fleece lined.

PATCHES

There's 16 different patches to choose from and some styles come in three different sizes and prices vary accordingly. You can even get a large Ace Cafe London back patch, in leather for £60.

TERRY DOBNEY

My introduction to the Ace came in 1959 when I was 10 years old. I lived in Aldershot and several families who all used to go to the same pub were invited to Granada TV studios to be the live audience for an edition of Michael Miles' Take Your Pick. It was meant to be a half-hour programme but filming took three hours so when we finished at 10pm on a Friday and got on the bus to come home, someone asked the driver if we could stop off for a cup of tea first. He said the only place still open was the Ace Cafe, just down the road, but warned us it was a 'bit rough' there.

No one seemed worried so off we went to the Ace and I can remember just hanging on the railings there watching all these bikes ripping up and down the road. All these ton-up boys. I can visualise it all now in black and white. I loved it.

By the time I was 14, I'd saved a few pounds and went to a local cafe in Aldershot where some of the bike lads hung out. I went in and offered to pay someone the petrol money to take me to the Ace. The only person to take up the offer was a lad they called Batty Bellhouse, the local bike looney. He had a bathtub Speed Twin and off we went. You don't have fear as a 14-year-old and he was riding like an absolute lunatic. It was still all black and white. And oil everywhere!

My first bike was a 1952 C11 250 BSA, the dynamo one, which I bought for £60. It had two and half gears – you could find second in there sometimes – and it had a leopard skin seat cover. The Ace was only 45 miles away and I'd ride over there on my own. I loved the place.

Later I bought a 1966 Black Shadow. My mates were all building motorways, earning big money and buying the latest bikes. I was on three quid as a motorbike mechanic and paid £125 for the Vincent. I also built a Triton using a Triumph GP engine in a Featherbed frame.

The Ace was about as rough as you could go in the 1960s. My local haunt was the Old Manor Cafe at Blackwater (on the A30 in Hampshire) and I'd go to the Cellar in Windsor but very few wanted to come to the Ace. It was open 24 hours and you'd have guys out the back selling dodgy gear, fights, prostitutes. That's why there was a spoon on a chain and all the chairs were bolted to the floor. I'd sit at one end of the Ace with my mates and watch it all going on. It was proper rock 'n' roll. And because of the way it was, it was full of really interesting characters.

I used to go to the 59 Club. You could get a cheap meal there then go to the Ace and stay all night until about 4am when it was getting light. Then you could ride home. You couldn't leave any earlier because your lights never worked. Good old Joe Lucas. We didn't have spare cash to fix our bikes anyway.

It's amazing, the Ace sells beer now. Imagine if it had in the 1960s – I'd never have left the place!

When the Ace re-opened I came back here on an Aermacchi 250 that I dragged out of a skip. It was untaxed, totally illegal but I roared across here and it was great to be back.

I think Mark (Wilsmore) has done an excellent job with the Ace. He lets boys be boys within certain parameters and I love the diversity of the bikes and people you get here these days.

I still come here once a month – and for the special occasions. I've had lots of different bikes over the years but I have a Guzzi V7 and a Victory that I ride – plus the old stuff. Got an Indian 101 in my living room. I've got nine Indians all together. I also have a very rare 1959 KHK that was hand-built in the Harley competition shop.

I reckon I've ridden over a million and a half miles. I've been riding since the age of 13, legally since 16 and I'm 65 now. I was hoping to make it two million but my legs are failing me. I've had so many operations over the years to fix the crash damage. I had a stroke a year ago and was paralysed down my left side. I'm okay now though and I can hold on to handlebars okay.

The BSA I rode here today is a 1940 side valve M20 that spent 27 years in the British Army. It's another bike I fished out of a skip full of rusty water. Cost me 200 quid to get the bike MoT'd and this is the third year I've had it on the road. I live in Avebury – I'm the Archdruid of Avebury, The Keeper Of The Stones – so it's a good ride here. I'm off to Spain this year on my Guzzi. Think I'll stop off at the factory in Italy on the way.

ACE WORLDWIDE

ACE CAFE AND THE
GERMAN CONNECTION

Since 1996 there has been growing interest in the Ace Cafe in Germany. Up till now, its home has been the road and cyberspace. Now that's all about to change with the potential for opening an Ace Cafe there next year. The man doing the groundwork is Hans Peter Rutten. He reveals the background story to the new development…

How did you become involved with the Ace in the first place?

I did an article about the Ace Cafe London for Motorrad (one of the leading German motorcycle magazines) in 1996. I'd heard about the cafe, went to London to do a reportage and met Mark Wilsmore. It was only a short time after the Reunion and it was early days but as well as going to the Ace, I went to Brighton and I was totally fascinated by the idea of the Ace Cafe, cafe racers and the heritage etc.

Wasn't the whole ton-up/rocker/cafe racer thing a strange phenomenon for a German?

I looked at the bikes, bikes like the Triumph Metisse, the Tritons, and thought they were rather cool. Even the two-valve BMW to me seemed a lot of fun as a cafe racer. Don't ask me why. It (the BMW) had two of everything – two cylinders, two carbs, two pipes. It was all rather symmetrical and seemed the perfect layout for a simple brain like mine!

What bike did you have?

In 1998 I started building my own cafe racer – based on a 90/6 BMW – clip-ons, solo seat, some work on the 'mufflers', decent tyres.

But what of your countrymen? Were they Ace Cafe devotees too?

At that time only a few Germans could deal with the idea of a cafe racer. You have to understand that the German language uses quite awkward terms for things – like 'handi' where the rest of the world uses 'mobile phone' or 'cell phone.' A cafe racer in German was seen as a derogatory term from someone who didn't go anywhere on their bike – and just rode from cafe to cafe. They didn't understand the concept of making street bikes that were stripped down and race tuned – and racing maybe from the Ace Cafe to a cafe in Brighton – or even up to Edinburgh!

What changed?

We had to fight to get people to understand. I wasn't exactly ostracized but I did have to explain my bike to many people. But I was bitten by the bug. I'd just started an internet company, which at the time was quite a new venture. I volunteered to do the Ace website – which I did from 1996 until 2007 until Mark launched the official Ace Cafe London site.

So what was the game plan between 1996 and 2007?

It was all about brand recognition. Being an internet site, it was global so the fact that it was run from Germany didn't matter. I remember Mark, Linda and myself going to the NEC Show one time and handing out leaflets – with me trying to convince people about this fantastic project to reopen the Ace – me telling Brits in my awkward German accent!

So when did Ace Cafe Germany officially start?

After the Ace reopened in 2001 the brand began to develop to what you see now. When the official Ace Cafe London site launched, I founded Ace Cafe GMBh with the task of gaining more brand awareness in Germany – always with the aim to eventually open Ace Cafe Germany. I've also got the licence to open Ace Cafe in Switzerland and Austria.

Right now there's no 'home' for the Ace Cafe Germany. Its home is the road. How close are we to a permanent cafe?

In 2003/4 it looked very possible to link with Hein Gericke and a site in Dusseldorf – until the old Hein Gericke company went into bankruptcy. We didn't lose money but we lost all the work we had put into the venture. Now we are once again close to opening our own Ace Cafe Germany.

Why has it taken so long?

In London there was the base on the North Circular that had history going back to 1938. In Germany we are starting from scratch. It would be easy to open 'franchises' all over – like

'I looked at the bikes, bikes like the Triumph Metisse, the Tritons, and thought they were rather cool. Even the two-valve BMW to me seemed a lot of fun as a cafe racer'

Above:
The Ace Cafe at Intermot. The biggest motorcycle show in Europe a corner of British culture

Below:
Home is where the heart is. And for Ace Cafe Germany, home is currently a travelling roadshow. It's not about buildings. It's about a state of mind.

McDonald's does, or Hard Rock Café, or any of those huge corporations. But Mark has said he'll never do that because it has to be authentic. It has to develop its own identity but with the black and white chequered tape and the rock and roll. You need that same feel when you go into Ace Cafe Hamburg as you do in Ace Cafe London. That's not easily done.

Seriously, what appetite is there for Ace Germany?

As I have said, we've worked on brand awareness and there are a couple of really good stories to suggest there is real growth in the Ace Cafe/cafe racer scene. In 1998 we started a party at Cafe Hubraum in Solingen. From there a group rode to Ace Cafe, London for the Reunion. Maybe it's 100-150 people. Each year it gets bigger and more and more people join us en route – to the point where we now need 4000 ferry bookings. If you go to Ace for the Reunion – out of the 10,000 weekend crowd, 10-15% will be from Europe.

And the other story?

In winter 2005/6 things really began to gain momentum. We had done shows like Dortmund, 130,000 people, but then this guy called Jorg Letzenberger came to see me. He already ran a small 'old timers' biker meet but struck on the idea of a new event, based on cafe racers, after seeing a Red Bull soap box derby at the Glemseck Hotel. After much nagging from him I checked out the site and it was on the old Solitude GP road racing circuit. I looked at the history and realised the potential.

It's arguably the best cafe racer event in the world.

Exactly. We worked with Jorg and Peter Haller at Leonburg city council. I made a programme for sponsors and for the show and it's taken off in a big way. I convinced the big manufacturers this would be a different kind of show – a way to promote the industry to a new breed of customer (the focus is on cafe racer customs plus a low-key 1/8th mile drag racing competition that's purely for fun but there's also a

huge bike show and bands, creating a really laid-back uber-cool atmosphere). We planned a 360° platform for the manufacturers, an event where they were all on show, all working together. And it's revived interest in motorcycling in Germany, the entire event based on the ethos of the cafe racer. I'm proud to say it's been driven by the Ace Cafe, with big help from Jorg and Peter Haller of course. It attracted 30,000 in the first year and continues to grow.

When I went to Glemseck for the first time last year, it seemed that the average age of the bikers was younger than we see in England. Is that a German cafe racer phenomenon?

I think that's very true. But you know it doesn't matter if it's a 1950s British single or an R1. Even if there are massive technical differences between the bikes, it's the spirit that's the same. If you embrace that Ace Cafe ton-up spirit (speed, passion, rock and roll) then you will enjoy an event like Glemseck 101.

So what's the future now for Ace Cafe Germany?

As I said we're looking at a permanent home. We have two potential sites: Berlin and Hamburg. We're a long way down the road with the latter and I'd hope we can make an announcement for 2014. We've still a lot of work ahead of use but I'm optimistic.

And beyond Germany?

I think you'll see an Ace Cafe in Zurich. There's an Ace Cafe in Beijing opening on September 26. Ace Cafe Orlando should open next Spring. And by 2015 I think you'll see several Ace Cafe's in cool places.

Bejing? How does that fit with Ace heritage, passion, cafe racers?

That's a very good question! I think we're about to discover the answer. It's going to be a very interesting experience.

The Ultimate
Riding Machine

BMW CONCEPT NINETY.
CLASSIC MEETS CLASS.

Celebrating 90 years of history – and 40 years of a BMW Motorrad design icon. In collaboration with Roland Sands Design, BMW Motorrad proudly present an exclusive tribute to the BMW R 90 S. Roland Sands and his team have crafted a motorcycle which echoes the iconic style and striking looks of the legendary racer, with its self-assured appearance and technologically refined, top-quality custom parts.

FOR MORE INFORMATION, PLEASE CONTACT YOUR LOCAL BMW MOTORRAD DEALER.

www.bmw-motorrad.co.uk
www.bmw-motorrad.ie

ACE WORLDWIDE

ACE CAFE STORMS
BMW MOTORRAD

The annual BMW Motorrad Days at Garmisch-Partenkirchen in July held special significance on three counts. It was the 90th Anniversary celebration of BMW Motorrad. The firm launched its Concept 90. And for first time, the Ace Cafe was invited to have its own stand.

"My personal view is that BMW launched Concept 90 there to pave the way for its production cafe racer-style bike that's coming end of September, early October," says Ace Germany's Hans Peter Rutten.

"When you look at BMW history, its bikes of the Seventies, Eighties and Nineties were not those of choice for many. The current GS range had limited appeal with Gortex and those helmets that lift up at the front.

"My view is that BMW wanted to do something different, something that harks back to the days of Georg Meier and the supercharged BMW GP bike (1939) – to create some real sex appeal – hence Concept 90.

"It's also my impression, that somewhere along the line, BMW bosses might have thought, 'we need bikes that are about passion, about heartbeat.' And that's why they looked

at Ace Cafe (BMW is involved in a big way with this year's Ace Cafe Reunion on September 13-15).

"I really think it will suit BMW well to have a real cafe racer like Concept 90 in its range and I think the company is thinking the same way too – though it might be presumptuous of me to suggest I have any idea of its marketing plans.

"Garmisch was interesting. As I said, lots of Gortex and funny helmets. Thousands of GS models. It was certainly a challenge for us to make an impression.

"The first thing was we refused one of the clinical white canopies – they said no branding allowed – and took our own black one with Ace livery! We organised a wall of death – and used it in the evening to form the backdrop for our rock 'n' roll bands!

"We were Ace Corner and late in the evening at 10pm, then 11pm and then midnight, the bosses of BMW kept coming by and were blown away not just with the huge party we had going on, but with the younger people we attracted, the new breed of cafe racers!"

ABOUT CONCEPT 90

To celebrate 90 years of BMW Motorrad, and pay homage to the BMW the R90S sportbike, BMW rolled out Concept 90 to its hardcore fans at Garmisch.

The machine was built in collaboration American custom builder Roland Sands but is based on the BMW R90S street bike launched in 1973.

The original R90S had a top speed of just under 200kph, making it one of the fastest production motorcycles of its time.

"The BMW R90S goes back to a time when motorcyclists were regarded as social outlaws. There was something rebellious about them – they were fast, noisy and wild. It was all about pure emotion. And it remains fascinating to this day," said Edgar Heinrich, head of BMW Motorrad Design.

The bike's basic proportions are clearly geared towards the original. The fairing, fuel tank and rear section instantly reveal a link with the BMW R90S.

Ola Stenegard, head of BMW Motorrad Vehicle Design, added: "The aim of the BMW Concept 90 is to show how reduced and pure an emotional BMW motorcycle can be."

Ace Cafe boss Mark Wilsmore was at Garmisch and got a close-up look at Concept 90. He said: "It's very bold – and brave. It's a great concept and I really hope they can take the design all the way to final production."

*BMW Motorrad is making the most of what appears to be an awesome brand position opportunity by bringing Concept 90 to the Ace Cafe Reunion. It'll also have several top brass on staff to discuss it and other BMW motorcycle topics with enthusiasts.

ACE RIDES

BIKERS...
AND THEIR BIKES

The Ace sees thousands of bikers coming and going all year round. Daytime, night-time, the bikes roll in and out. Every rider, every bike has a story. Here are just a few of the great characters giving the background to the bike they rode to the Ace when we happened to be there...

MARK PHILLIPS
1963 TRITON

I've had the bike 23 years. At 17 years old I built a Rocket Gold Star that I'd bought in boxes but sold it before I took my test. Then I bought this bike, the same year I got married. The bike came early in the year and I got married in summer. It's still my only bike, though there have been threats of buying something else.

The engine is a 1956 pre-unit with Morgo 750cc barrels, lightened timing wheels, Thruxton camshafts. It had all the mods when I bought it but my priority was to get the engine out and tidy it up.

I changed the clutch originally by fitting heavier springs but they were too heavy so I went for an LP Williams conversion. It's still a four-spring clutch but you get an extra plate which improves the friction – and it gives a smoother operation.

Gearbox is a four-speed Slickshift. I was going to swap it for a five-speed to improve the cruising speed but I don't think it's worth the effort. The bike is really strong away from the lights.

The frame is a 1963 Wideline. It was painted blue when I got it and, originally I was tempted to paint it black – but everyone has got black frames so I kept it as it was. In fact, the rolling chassis is pretty much as I bought it. Even the swingarm is stock. It's got short Norton Roadholders and a Commando twin-leading shoe front brake. I know some people go for four-leading shoe Italian brakes which might have a bit more bite but they're not so period. That's the thing for me, I like to keep it looking period.

I recovered the original grey seat but I used fishing line to stitch up the thick covering and had to make my own thimble from a pipe-fitting and a penny to push the needle through the fabric! It had to be done and you learn ways of doing new things.

I also laced up both wheels recently. I decided to fit new stainless spokes – to make cleaning the thing a bit easier – and that was really satisfying once I got the job done. I had to do one wheel twice – first time around the spokes had been labelled wrongly.

The rear brake pedal is a good talking point. When Brodie, my daughter was born I drew around her foot and made a brake pedal to that shape. It was a way to commemorate her birth. Now my son Riley is always asking "where's my bit on the bike?"

Originally the bike came with a three gallon fuel tank but this one is now just under five. It's actually to fit a Slimline frame so it comes up shorter and shows more of the frame rails, which I like. It was originally pinstriped but I got the paint stripper out and really like the polished look.

I do love cleaning the bike (*it looks so clean it could be a freshly built machine – Editor*). It's the only way to really know your machine. I've heard people say it's so clean I can't ever ride it but it's not true, I ride it a lot. People also say a Triton is never finished, that you always look to alter things and that's true in some ways. I've even changed the engine plates since I've owned it to alter the way the engine sits in the frame – just to get it looking right. It's always a labour of love.

The Ace is a horrible ride from my place but I get down there on a regular basis. I've known Mark for many years – we used to meet up at the Triumph Owners Club and I remember he was always talking about reopening the Ace. Then one day, blow me down, he went and did it!

MARTYN SPEIRS
2005 HOGBITZ SPORTSTER

I was sitting outside the Ace one day and Brian from Hogbitz rode up on a Harley 1400cc cafe racer. I'd seen him and his bikes at a few shows before but this time I thought, 'I have to have one of those'.

It's been two years in the making but I'm so pleased with it. I've also got a BMW RT1200 – and I've had three GS BMWs in the past too – in fact I've had BMs for the past 15 years.

I was worried the clip-ons and rear-sets on the Sportster might make it excruciatingly uncomfortable but it's so easy to ride. The steering is quite neutral and the brakes are adequate. The engine is beautiful – with a Stage 2 tune.

This is a 2005 donor bike, that started life as an 883 but is now 1200cc – it's registered as an 883 Sportster, with 1200cc barrels – but still with 883 gearing.

I think it's a stock carb but the air cleaner is by Forcewinder.

This was the first rubber-mounted Sportster Brian had done and he had to modify the rear of the frame to take the wider-section tyre. Being a Harley, I'd heard all the talk and really expected it to vibrate but it's so smooth to ride.

When I made the initial order, I gave Brian two foolscap pages of what I wanted – it was so detailed, even down to the size of the holes drilled in the chain guard.

He wanted to build it with an 'abbreviated' front mudguard. I wanted a full front mudguard.

The front end is Sportster with a twin disc set-up. The only things unmodified on the bike are the front brakes, handlebar levers, engine bottom end, transmission and rear brake.

It has two-into-one header pipes with a single Gold Star exhaust, which sounds nice. The rearset pegs are by Storz pegs and it's a Storz master cylinder too.

Tyres are Avon 150/70V18 rear and 11/80V18 front. Shocks are by Hagon.

It's a tribute to a Norvin or an Egli Vincent (the style is indeed reminiscent of the Swiss-built Egli). It's H-D but I feel it's missing the R, between the other two initials! But (Martyn says, looking for some wood to touch!) with this bike comes modern reliability.

STUART OSBORNE
1965 TRIUMPH BONNEVILLE

My bike was built by George Hopwood – the only bloke I'd buy a pre-built bike from. He's a real gentleman.

I went on the net three years ago looking for rocker gaskets and this came up. I bought it from Parkside Classics.

It was sold as a 'Thruxton replica' – a Sixties version of an Ace boy's Thruxton. But you don't need high performance for the road these days so it's got a 750cc big bore kit and that's about it.

I grew up in Feltham Football Club – well, in the rock 'n' roll club there. I'm still into the music now. We have a band called the Guana Batz – it's like bastardised rock 'n' roll, crossed with punk – it's called 'psychobilly.' Two of the band live in the States now but we still tour and played in Japan back in January this year.

Psychobilly was big when I was 15 years old, when The Meteors came out and kicked off a whole new scene that meant kids had a music they could call their own.

I'm 48 now but was into cars as a kid – Mk.II Consuls and the like. I didn't get into bikes until I was 26, which was good in a way because I had some road sense by then.

I used to ride a Guzzi 750T to Waterloo every day but traded that in for a Dresda Triumph in 1996 when I got a company car with my job.

I've been to the TT on the Dresda – thrashed it over the Mountain at over 100mph several times. Thrashed it home then rebuilt it.

We recreated The Leatherboys Run one year, my mate John on a bitza A10 cafe racer with a fairing. Me on my 1965 Bonnie. We'd seen the film and just wanted to see what we could recognise from the film.

These days, so many people cosset their old bikes. The Leatherboys Run was 410 miles each way and we did about 70-75mph all the way on the open roads. We were going to do it again this year but work commitments ruled it out. There's always next year.

GRAHAM
1952 TRIUMPH THUNDERBIRD

I love the sleek styling of this particular model. To me it's the most classic of the Edward Turner-designed Triumphs.

I love the colour too and those blue bars – the bend is as fitted to the US spec bikes – were for one year only. The Speed Twins were the same and it's because in 1952 there was a shortage of nickel due to the Korean War. It meant all the bolts on the bikes were cadmium plated, the wheels were painted silver instead of being chrome and the handlebars were painted blue.

I wanted the bike to be finished as if it rolled out of the factory in 1952, hence the paint finish.

I've also got a 1956 Trophy, which I restored but about the only thing I've done on this bike is the polishing! I asked Cliff of Ace Classics to source me the bike and believe it or not it came as a previously restored machine. However, I'm too much of a perfectionist and thought it either has to be authentic or fully restored so I got Ace Classics to do the work and it also provided a lot of the original parts – including the Lucas parts.

I did the West Kent Run on it a couple of weeks ago and covered 240 miles. Mind you, it broke down 10 miles into the ride. There were flames out of the exhaust and I thought my weekend was ruined but I had one spanner in my pocket and it fitted the magneto. The nut in the middle of the points had come loose and the (points) gap had closed up. Once I got that sorted the bike never missed a beat. It's beautiful to ride. Great weekend but it got filthy and it took a lot of elbow grease to restore its looks.

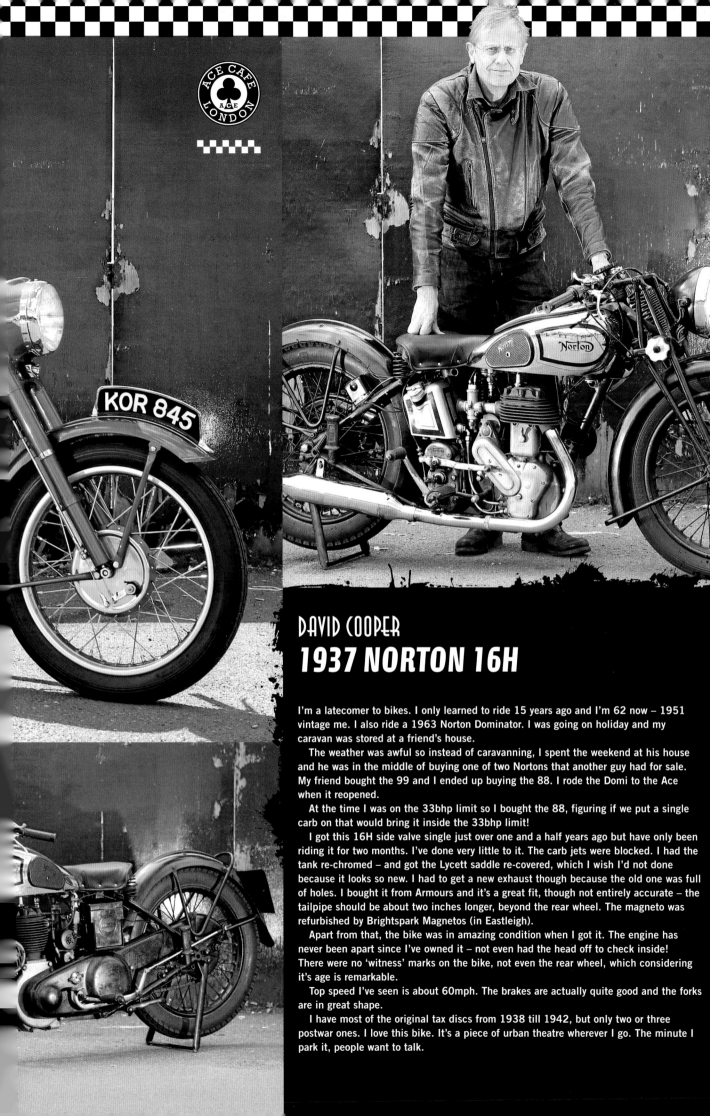

DAVID COOPER
1937 NORTON 16H

I'm a latecomer to bikes. I only learned to ride 15 years ago and I'm 62 now – 1951 vintage me. I also ride a 1963 Norton Dominator. I was going on holiday and my caravan was stored at a friend's house.

The weather was awful so instead of caravanning, I spent the weekend at his house and he was in the middle of buying one of two Nortons that another guy had for sale. My friend bought the 99 and I ended up buying the 88. I rode the Domi to the Ace when it reopened.

At the time I was on the 33bhp limit so I bought the 88, figuring if we put a single carb on that would bring it inside the 33bhp limit!

I got this 16H side valve single just over one and a half years ago but have only been riding it for two months. I've done very little to it. The carb jets were blocked. I had the tank re-chromed – and got the Lycett saddle re-covered, which I wish I'd not done because it looks so new. I had to get a new exhaust though because the old one was full of holes. I bought it from Armours and it's a great fit, though not entirely accurate – the tailpipe should be about two inches longer, beyond the rear wheel. The magneto was refurbished by Brightspark Magnetos (in Eastleigh).

Apart from that, the bike was in amazing condition when I got it. The engine has never been apart since I've owned it – not even had the head off to check inside! There were no 'witness' marks on the bike, not even the rear wheel, which considering it's age is remarkable.

Top speed I've seen is about 60mph. The brakes are actually quite good and the forks are in great shape.

I have most of the original tax discs from 1938 till 1942, but only two or three postwar ones. I love this bike. It's a piece of urban theatre wherever I go. The minute I park it, people want to talk.

HIROKO MURAKAMI
1948 TRIUMPH SPEED TWIN

I first came to England 23 years ago, when I was 20 years old, and fell in love with everything that was British. I like British bikes because I like all old things – antiques, buildings, fashions.

At 23 I decided I wanted to ride bikes, even though I'd not seen any other women riding bikes in Japan. I got my licence but had no idea of British bikes so I bought an old Honda CB250. Then I met a friend on a bike and he told me about old motorcycles and I fell in love with British bikes from the 1950s. In Japan I had a Tiger 90 and a Bantam.

I kept coming back to England every year, just to spend a holiday, then in 2000 I came to stay. I bought myself a 1961 BSA C15 and rode it for years. I love that little bike – it's so loud! I rode it to the Isle of Man TT in

2003. It's really good fun and I still have it, though it needs some work now.

I work at Vivien of Holloway, making 1950s reproduction dresses and other clothing. And I have my own brand called Ace of Speed which is some small accessories and T-shirts.

I bought the Triumph in August 2004. It is actually a 1948 model – but it looks like 1950 model. I do all my own routine maintenance – just the small things. I don't know about engines though. But this is a very reliable bike. One time I had some timing gears break but otherwise it's been very good.

If I could have another bike it would have to be an A10 BSA – late 1950s – early 1960s. I love that period of British motorcycles.

MARK PHILLIPS
1999 DEUS KAWASAKI W650

I'm 53 and semi retired, so I've started to collect bikes that I like.

I've been into bikes since I had a Bantam D7 as a kid. I sorted that and then in 1976 bought a Fantic Caballero – I was into the Italian crowd. I got an RD400 next and had numerous bike in that period.

In 1986 I bought a Virago. Someone pulled up beside me on a Harley and totally ignored me. That was it. I bought my first Harley in 1989. Then I had Jerry Cartwright of Peninsula Motor Cycles build me a T110 Wideline cafe racer. It was a classic cafe racer at a time when no one was doing anything like that. Then I got a drink driving year ban and sold it. But it's always been in my blood since then.

2010 I got back into the cafe racer thing and now I have a couple of BMW cafe racers and just bought a Seeley Honda.

This though, is a hooligan thing. Change the knobbly tyres and it would be a scream to ride on the road.

I think you're going to see a lot of Deus bikes now there's a shop just opened in Milan. This one is a 1999 W650, built in Sydney by Deus, and is one of the 'standard' models. It was imported here two years ago by John Teeman and it's an early incarnation of the Deus.

I bought it because of its rarity. I like to be the first kid on the block.

When you look at it, it would be easy to build something similar – I could have done it myself but I like the whole Deus lifestyle thing – the clothing, the surfing. The brand appeals to me.

There was talk at one stage that John, Charley Boorman and Nicholas Cowell (yes, the brother of that Cowell) were going to become Deus importers (under the Dukes Emporium banner), looking at a West London site; boutique, hotel, restaurant, gallery, motorcycles – something that would appeal to any petrolhead. But the project is on hold at the moment.

The Deus is great to ride. When I first got it, the motor was set up for the crap Australian petrol – they only have 87Ron. We have 95-97. So once we got it here, we set the thing up on PDQ's dyno and it runs like a dream now.

The tyres are not great (Heidenau 110-80B 19MC front and 140-80 x 18 rear). If it had supermoto tyres it would be stupid (mad) to ride! It's very comfortable. Very reliable. And very economical. Parts are easy to obtain – if, god forbid, I ever need them.

I think Deus has taken the W650 and shown the true potential of a bike Kawasaki has produced for the mass market.

STEVE HILLARY
1980 KNIGHT NORTON

I run the Red Max Speedshop, specialising in flat track racing equipment and cafe racers and I raced this Norton on British tracks in the Dirt Track Racing Association until I broke my leg rather badly.

I was racing an XR750 Harley. It's a bike built for half-miles and miles in the USA but the long wheelbase wasn't suited to the short tracks we race on here. I'd get the holeshot then miss apexes.

I also had a 1980s Knight-framed Bultaco but I don't really like two-strokes and I'm a big fan of Norton anyway. So I looked at the Commando engine I had in a cafe racer and thought, 'this might fit but the gearbox won't. So I run the bike with no gearbox and run it through a speedway countershaft.

The bike is five inches shorter than the Harley, two thirds of the weight and wheelies for England. It's a 920cc motor with high-lift cams and flatslide carbs."

DEUS – THE CULTURE

Just like the Ace Cafe, Deus Ex Machina has earned iconic status within motorcycling culture.

The company was the brainchild of Australian Dare Jennings, who grew up surfing and biking, and co-founded Mambo surfware in the 1980s – which was sold in 2000 for 'more than $20million'.

Jennings then developed Deus Ex Machina (god from the machine), which says the Deus website, 'roared into Australia's cultural consciousness in 2006, with some neatly customised motorcycles and a quaint notion that doing something is more fun than just owning something'.

Deus Ex Machina reckons it is 'a step bigger than a brand' and has become a culture – which is probably true. Since the company's arrival on the scene – it could be argued, with some inspiration from Japanese custom bike shops like Brat Style – the whole cafe racer/streetracker/bobber phenomenon has exploded across the globe and no matter where you look on the web now, there are bikes being built in a similar vein to the original offerings from Deus.

So it's no surprise that Deus Ex Machina claims its showroom/cafe/headquarters in Sydney has 'immediately become a shrine to 'run-what-you-brung' resourcefulness and street-honest industrial art'.

The style that taps into various cultures – motorcycling, surfing, skateboarding, and BMX – has brought a vibrant new culture to the motorcycling world – and Mark Phillips, in turn, has brought it to the Ace!

PAUL MANSELL
1974 CHAMPION YAMAHA XS650

The late Tony Hall of Halco (Europe's premier XS650 tuning specialist parts supplier until Tony's untimely death) found the bike in New Mexico back in 1996. It's of 1974/75 origin and features a chrome moly Champion frame, with Barnes rear hub and QD sprocket, Progressive rear springs. Forks are by Ceriani but I rebuilt the front wheel using a Talon hub. The motor has a 750 race kit and is fed by twin 34mm Dell'Orto carbs.

The two-stroke single bike is a DT360, circa 1972, similar to the bike Kenny Roberts would have raced on the short tracks (dirt ovals of quarter-mile or less) and also has a Champion frame with Airheart rear caliper and twin Koni shocks. This particular DT360 engine has a 35bhp seven-port motocross barrel. I found the bike in Essex. The owner used to ride around the fields and had no idea of its origins.

MIKE & SCOTT HAYWOOD
1949 SUNBEAM S8 & 1960 MATCHLESS G12CSR

Mike: I've been an Ace regular since 1962. I've owned this Sunbeam six years and have seven other vintage bikes.

I've had S7 or S8s since I was 16. I just like them because they are a little bit different to the run of mill Triumph, BSA and Norton. I've done a lot of work on this one, but it was in reasonably good condition when I bought it.

It's nice and smooth to ride, handles well and cruises at 50-60mph. You can't push these any harder anyway because they pump all the oil out!

Scott: I'm 23 now but I first came to the Ace 15 years ago on the back of dad's T120 Bonnie.

I've had this Matchless for eight weeks. I swapped an M31 AJS for it. The Ajay is a very similar bike but I just wanted an earlier model twin.

I've also got a 1965 T120 and a 1993 Moto Guzzi V1000, which I use for work. The vintage bikes are purely for pleasure. All my mates ride modern crap because most of them are only interested in speed. If I want a mad moment or two I can take the Guzzi but if I want a more sedate pleasurable ride, I've got my old bikes.

It's a BSA A10 in an A7 frame. When I bought the engine as a basket case 25 years ago it was in a 1956 plunger frame. I was looking for a rigid frame that was untampered with and found one in Wales.

Front end with disc brake is off a T140. Rear is an A7 brake hub. I put 16in rims on to take those fat tyres.

I had BSA Bantams, C15s and B40s in the Seventies and I think the A10 motor is beautiful. It's a fantastic motor. Mine's standard apart from a Rocket Gold Star head. It's got a belt primary and 16-plate clutch.

I know guys who will spend £700 just for fancy bars with internal wiring but you can get an A10 rebuilt for that!

I've also got a Triumph T120 that's built for London roads. It's got plenty of steering lock on it – you need that in the city. And you need to see the road so I've an uprated (12 volt single-phased AC) alternator on the A10 from Alton in France and fitted a halogen headlight. Next upgrade will be Bike Viz daytime running lights. I learned from driving in India that loud horns are important too.

I just like to ride my bikes and I use the A10 daily around town. A lot of people put their classics away but do the right things to old British bikes and they are great for London's roads.

CHRIS BALL
1946 INDIAN CHIEF

My first big bike was a WLA Harley. Then I had an Indian Chief – I was 18 years old and I had no idea what it really was. I bought it in ignorance at the time – and sold it for a song too. Those days bikes like that were worth very little but I always regretted selling it.

My wife eventually got fed up with me moaning about it and told me to go and buy one. I found this one in Montana. I saw it in an advert in a magazine. It was going for $3400, which wasn't cheap at the time.

I did the entire deal over the phone. I sent the guy the money. He sent me the bike. Imagine that happening these days.

I've owned it 30 years now and it's part of the family. It's the only bike I have. I'm not a collector, I'm a user and I love riding this bike. It's reliable, extremely comfortable and I've got a bad left wrist so the foot clutch is perfect for me.

I've had other bikes over the years, BMWs etc., but they've all come and gone. But I'd never part with this. You can still buy them of course but they are not usually original like this one.

It's incredibly reliable. I've never had the engine apart and it's the same clutch that was in there when I bought it. It's got a four-row primary chain. That thing will never wear out. It's an incredible machine.

I took it back to the USA six years ago and rode it from Chicago to LA. Friends warned me not to take it into LA so I stopped at Riverside, California and spent a week with an Indian dealer there. He was a retired guy with a shed load of parts for bikes like this.

Fifteen years ago I had a front end smash with this bike. It snapped a few pins in the forks but the bike was otherwise unscathed. The car was a write off!

I ride all year round and I've been to Indian rallies in Europe. But as soon as I get there, I want to get back on and ride. I can't be sitting around a camp site. Likewise I like to ride alone. That way I can stop off when I like and have nothing to worry about. It's great fun riding this thing and it puts a smile on my face every time I fire it up.

PETROLHEADS

PHOTOS BY *MYKEL NICOLAOU, PHIL MASTERS AND ACE CAFE*
▪▪▪▪

Bikes or cars, the Ace has earned a worldwide reputation as being the mecca for petrolheads. The Ace Cafe website bears a message that says it all: "At Ace Cafe London we welcome all who share our passion, based upon the traditions of motorcycles, cars and rock 'n' roll. This is your cafe, devised, designed and built by fellow petrolheads, so enjoy the ambience and make the most of the facilities and activities to ensure that its history lives on."

The headline events are well known: The Ace Reunion and Brighton Burn-Up, The Southend Shakedown, The Margate Meltdown, The Wembley Stunt Fest and Streetfighter Show.

However, aside from the special events, there are meetings virtually every night of the week, and specials like Triton Day, Diamond Day at weekends – but it's not so much the bikes or cars that define those meets, it's the people who make them really special.

As the Ace says, those with the passion for motorcycles, cars and rock 'n' roll. So, over the final few pages of the Ace Cafe 75th Anniversary Special, we've gone back through several years of Ace-related archived pictures to create this tribute to the people who make the Ace what it is… the greatest home for petrolheads worldwide.

ACE TEAM

This is just one shift of the Ace Cafe crew. And this was one very rare quiet moment when there were a few seconds to get the entire crew together for one quick snap! Nice work gang. Now where's my bacon sarnie? Left to right: Romulda, Frank, Ewa, Marek, Anne Marie, Agnieszka, Michael, Vasilis, Mark Wilsmore, Stacey, Mario, Azizul, Pablo, Slawek. **PHOTO:** *MYKEL NICOLAOU*